The
HERB
Handbook

*An illustrated
guide to growing,
harvesting and
using herbs.*

Pamela Westland

GALLERY BOOKS
An Imprint of W. H. Smith Publishers Inc.
112 Madison Avenue
New York City 10016

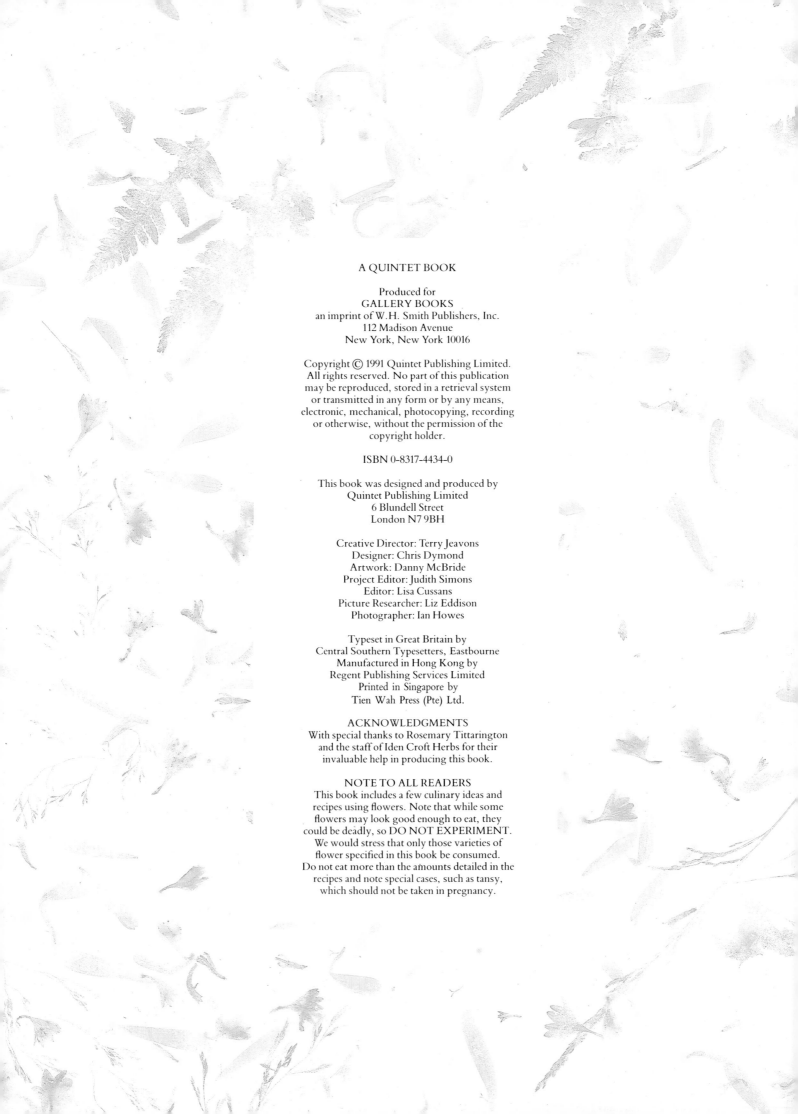

A QUINTET BOOK

Produced for
GALLERY BOOKS
an imprint of W.H. Smith Publishers, Inc.
112 Madison Avenue
New York, New York 10016

ISBN 0-8317-4434-0

This book was designed and produced by
Quintet Publishing Limited
6 Blundell Street
London N7 9BH

Creative Director: Terry Jeavons
Designer: Chris Dymond
Artwork: Danny McBride
Project Editor: Judith Simons
Editor: Lisa Cussans
Picture Researcher: Liz Eddison
Photographer: Ian Howes

Typeset in Great Britain by
Central Southern Typesetters, Eastbourne
Manufactured in Hong Kong by
Regent Publishing Services Limited
Printed in Singapore by
Tien Wah Press (Pte) Ltd.

ACKNOWLEDGMENTS
With special thanks to Rosemary Tittarington
and the staff of Iden Croft Herbs for their
invaluable help in producing this book.

NOTE TO ALL READERS
This book includes a few culinary ideas and
recipes using flowers. Note that while some
flowers may look good enough to eat, they
could be deadly, so DO NOT EXPERIMENT.
We would stress that only those varieties of
flower specified in this book be consumed.
Do not eat more than the amounts detailed in the
recipes and note special cases, such as tansy,
which should not be taken in pregnancy.

Contents

Introduction

People have made use of herbs since the beginning of time. Even before they learned to hunt, primitive people depended on herbs for both food and medicine, using them to add flavor to grain-based dishes and, later, as preservatives for meat and fish. Herbs were regarded so highly they assumed importance in religious rites and festivals, and many superstitions grew up around them.

The earliest record of the use of herbs is an Egyptian papyrus, dating from around 2000 BC, that mentions the existence of herb doctors, while it is known that herbs played an important role in all of the world's ancient civilizations. In India and China, where herbal remedies formed a large part of medicinal practice, many ancient remedies are still prescribed today by natural healers and practitioners of holistic medicine. The works of the great philosophers and physicians of Ancient Greece – Hippocrates in the third century BC with his herbal, *De Materia Medica*, and Dioscorides,

c AD 60 – put hundreds of herbs into their botanical and medicinal context; and herbs are frequently mentioned in both the old and new testaments of the Bible. The Romans made such lavish use of herbs in both medicines and highly spiced dishes, the plants were an indispensable part of their equipment wherever they traveled. Indeed, it is said the success of the advancing Roman armies was attributed largely to their knowledge and use of herbs. All countries once Roman colonies have the Romans to thank for many of the herbs grown and used there today. The Roman scholar Pliny (AD 23–79) documented the extensive use of herbs in his many books on medicinal plants.

With the decline of the ancient cultures the use of herbs passed into oblivion, only to re-emerge in the Middle Ages when they were cultivated in monasteries and in the gardens of great estates. The monks put herbs to both medicinal and culinary use, and eventually the knowledge spread into the towns and villages so

RIGHT: A painting of a late 14th-century herb garden, showing the formality of the geometric design popular in medieval times.

OPPOSITE LEFT: Illustrated herbals abounded in the 18th century. This illustration is taken from a book by T. Sheldrake published in 1759, called *Botanicum medicinale*.

OPPOSITE RIGHT: An early 20th-century engraving by F. Delpech, after Vernet, shows a street herb seller offering sheaves of bay leaves and strings of garlic.

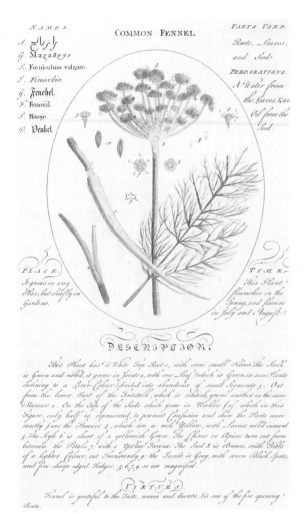

people could grow their own self-help remedies. In the grander houses, herbs were used for pot pourri as well as for strewing on floors to sweeten the atmosphere.

During this time many erudite works were written and published, setting out the characteristics and uses of a great many herbal plants. William Turner (1508–79), a doctor and a clergyman, wrote a comprehensive *Herball* based on his scientific background. John Gerard (b 1545), who was the keeper of Lord Burghley's gardens in England, a surgeon, and apothecary to James I, wrote his herbal from practical experience. He formed a collection of medicinal and other plants from all over the world, and wrote about them with passion and understanding. And then there was Nicholas Culpeper, whose herbal set out to identify the medicinal plants and define their uses. He was a follower of a form of natural healing known as the Doctrine of Signatures, which teaches that like cures like; that red flowers, for example, are most likely to cure disorders of the blood.

Already well established in the medicine chest, herbs gradually came to be used more and more in cooking – as flavorings, in sauces, as preservatives, and as vegetables. This knowledge of the use of herbs spread throughout Europe, and was taken to North America

by the early settlers. Here, it was the Shaker communities that first made a successful commercial enterprise out of growing, drying, and selling herbs.

By the nineteenth century the use of herbs had fallen into decline. People no longer needed to grow herbs for domestic medicines when they could buy synthetic substitutes in the form of modern drugs. With modern storage and preserving techniques, herbs were no longer needed to preserve food, nor to mask undesired flavors, and people simply stopped growing them. Indeed, until only recently, four herbs – parsley, thyme, mint, and chives – represented the sum total of most herb gardens.

Times have changed, the pendulum has swung back, and there is currently a strong revival of interest in these versatile plants. People have again become aware of the advantages of natural produce grown in an organic way. Cooks are ever more adventurous, experimenting with a wide range of exotic dishes requiring a large variety of herbs to flavor them. Not since the Middle Ages has there been such a wealth of interest in growing and using herbs. It is hoped this book will provide the inspiration to encourage this interest still further.

Carle Vernet
Marchand de Lauriers
du laurier de l'œil

CHAPTER 1

How To Grow Herbs

Growing herbs is one of the most delightful aspects of gardening. The plants are pleasantly fragrant, mostly decorative, some are highly colorful, and the majority can be used in the kitchen or around the home. Added to that, herbs are among the easiest plants to grow, so herb gardening is the ideal springboard for new and inexperienced gardeners. Can you ask for anything more!

Planning an herb garden is the first exciting stage in a continuing process that may well become a fascinating hobby. Whether you have a patch of garden you can give over to herbs, a border or two to which some herbs can be added, or simply a site for a few herb-filled pots and planters, it makes little difference: growing herbs will be a fulfilling and rewarding pastime.

Most herbs originate in the sunny climate of the Mediterranean and other warm regions elsewhere and have been reluctantly introduced to colder climes. This being the case, the first requirement is to find a sunny spot for them where, if possible, they can be in the sun for at least five or six hours a day. There are a few shade-loving herbs specified in the Directory in the later pages of this book, and these can be planted in the shadow of taller plants, or beside a wall or fence.

If you live in an area where cold winds are a more frequent feature than warm sunshine, this does not mean you cannot grow herbs successfully. Choose the most sheltered spot you can find, erect some kind of windbreak if you can, and be prepared to keep tender young plants under a glass or plastic cloche or frame.

If you are spoiled for choice and have two or three suitable spots, choose the one closest to the house. On an emotional level, it is one of life's greatest luxuries to have scented plants close to a window, where you can get a heart-lifting waft of the fragrance. On a practical level, you are much more likely to gather a few herb leaves on a rainy day if you don't need to wear rubber boots and a raincoat to do it.

It is a good idea to draw a scale plan of your designated plot, draw in any existing or proposed paths, and then allocate the space to the herbs you choose. The "characteristics" information in the Directory, giving the possible height and spread of each plant, will help you decide which herbs you can accommodate. Try to make your choice a happy compromise between those herbs you will use frequently in the kitchen, those you may want to learn about, those that are specially attractive to look at and, perhaps, others that are known to be attractive to bees.

You may decide to emulate the style of the monastery gardens and the Elizabethan knot gardens, with the herbs planted in regular geometric shapes and separated by bricks or compact, low-growing plants such as dwarf lavender. Or, in a completely different mood, you might decide to follow the style of a cottage garden,

growing a very informal mix of plant types in seemingly random order. It is a matter of personal preference – and the style of the rest of your garden – which you choose.

Most of the herbs you will grow fall neatly into two categories, annual and perennial, with a few biennials and others, such as bay, that are shrubs. Whichever garden style you choose, where possible separate annuals and perennials so you will not disturb the ongoing plants at the end of the season, when you clear the ground of annuals. Plan to site the tallest plants at the back of the border or in the center of an island bed, with low-growing plants at the front, where they can form a decorative edging. In a formal layout, group several of each plant type together so they form a mass. In an informal setting, group plants in clusters that blend one into the other.

Take not only height and width but also color and texture into consideration as you build up your plan, and create exciting visual effects by blending silver-leaved plants with purple leaves; yellow leaves with dark green; matte leaves alongside glossy ones; plain leaves beside fernlike or heavily cut ones. In this way, each of the herbs you choose will be seen to its most pleasing effect, and each will draw attention to its neighbor. Whoever said an herb garden was green!

If your herb garden does not extend to a patch of ground, but is simply given over to a few pots and tubs, plan it just as carefully, or perhaps even more carefully. Every tiny space in the container must be used effectively in terms of usefulness, fragrance, and appearance, and there is no room for the untidy luxury of straggly or unkempt plants.

OPPOSITE: This delightful corner of a scented garden shows two completely different ways to grow herbs to dramatic effect. On the one hand the plants are tumbling cottage-garden style along a walled border, and on the other they are neatly clipped in the formal manner of the great medieval estates.

BELOW: Closely planted clusters of colorful herbaceous flowers, soft hummocks of aromatic plants and the juxtaposition of contrasting leaves make for a lively border packed with interest.

PREPARING THE GROUND

The way you prepare the ground will have a significant effect on the health and quality of your plants for years to come, so it is well worth taking a little time and trouble at this stage. Good soil is essential for the success of most plants, although there are a few that are so persistent, they will flourish even in poor, under-nourished soil. Most herbs have a common dislike, that of sitting in damp soil with their roots permanently wet, so good drainage is essential. You can easily test the effective drainage of your soil by watering it and taking note. If the water remains on the surface and does not sink in, the soil has too much clay. If, on the following day, the soil is wet only to the surface 1 in/2.5 cm, then chances are it is too sandy.

If you are starting an herb garden from scratch, you should first dig it over to a depth of 12 in/30 cm, the comfortable depth achieved with a garden spade. If possible, dig in a 6-in/15-cm layer of compost or peat moss to improve the aeration of the soil and redress any deficiencies. This helps to hold the moisture in sandy soils and facilitates drainage in heavy clay, thus giving the roots air – the oxygen they need – and room to grow. If drainage is very poor, you can add perlite granules in the proportion recommended on the packet.

Most herbs have one other preference, that of a neutral or slightly alkaline soil. If you happen to know the pH factor of your soil, herbs like it to be around 6 to 7.5. If you do not know where your soil stands on this soil-test gauge, but suspect it is over acid, dig in some lime with the humus. Also, to get the herbs off to the best possible start, it is best to add in a dressing of organic fertilizer; there are several environment-friendly brands on the market now, and most garden centers have a good selection.

If you have decided on a formal layout for your herb plot – and by "formal" we do not mean "large" or "grand" – now is the time to stake it out with pegs and string, drawing in the straight lines or circles the herbs are to form. This way you can easily arrange the plants in the patterns they are to take, an especially pleasing sight from a window.

PLANTS OR SEEDS?

Once you have made your selection of the plants you want to grow, there is one more decision to take: whether to buy nursery-grown plants or to ask friends for root divisions, layered stems, and so on.

In general, annuals are the quickest and easiest to grow from seed. At its simplest, you plant the seed in pots, trays, or a well-prepared seed bed once the soil has warmed up in spring, water it well, and the seedlings will appear a few days later. But even so, you might prefer the concept of "instant gardening," and opt to buy plants of annuals as well as others.

SOWING SEEDS INDOORS

1 Gather together everything you need, clean pots, soil, seeds and labels, before you start.

2 Put in a layer of broken crocks, then loosely fill the pots with soil and lightly firm it to within ¼ in/6 mm of the rim.

3 Tip some seeds into your hand and sow them thinly over the surface, or shake them evenly from the corner of the packet.

4 Make sure that you do not sow the seeds too thickly, so that the seedlings will be over crowded when they germinate.

5 Sprinkle a thin layer of soil to cover the seeds and keep them permanently moist but not soaking.

6 Use a fine sprinkler for watering. Cover the seeds with a piece of glass or plastic and keep them warm.

If you decide to grow from seed, you can choose whether to sow the seed outdoors in a prepared seed bed or indoors in pots or trays. A seed bed should be completely free of weeds and stones, and raked until the soil is fine and crumbly – what gardeners call a "fine tilth." To sow seed outdoors in spring, however, it is essential to wait until there is no further danger of frost, and until the soil has had several days of sun to warm it. You can cheat a little by placing glass or plastic cloches over the soil before planting; this traps all the heat and does a good job of warming the soil.

By sowing seeds indoors, either in the home or in a greenhouse, you can advance the date by two or three weeks, thus getting the seedlings established earlier. You can sow seed in seed trays or in pots. Peat pots or peat blocks are ideal, especially for new gardeners: once the seedlings are established, they can be set out in the garden as they are, complete, without disturbing the roots. With trays or regular pots, use any good potting soil and be sure it is evenly moist. One way to do this is to cut a corner of the bag and pour in water, working it in to thoroughly dampen the soil – a horticultural game of mud pies. Fill the pots with the damp soil to within ½ in/12 mm of the top, and press it down gently. All roots need lightly compressed soil to enable them to take hold. Sow the seeds at the depth directed on the packet, rake a little soil over the top, and pat it down well. When sowing very fine seed, mix it with a little dry sand to distribute it evenly and guard against sowing too thickly.

Stand pots on a waterproof tray of sand or granules. Cover both seed trays and pots with a sheet of plastic to help retain moisture, and water them daily, so they never dry out. Remove the plastic covering once the seedlings appear, and put them in the sunniest place you can find. When the seedlings have taken root you can water pots from below, pouring water into the trays rather than over the pots.

Thin seedlings so those remaining have a chance to develop, and prick out those growing in seed trays into regular pots. There should be about 1 in/2.5 cm of soil all around the tiny roots.

At this stage, the seedlings benefit from a light feed with half-strength organic fertilizer every other day. Once they have developed two pairs of leaves, pinch out the tops to encourage bushy growth and the formation of branches. When the plants are several inches high and look healthy and strong, accustom them to the great outdoors by putting them in the garden, on the balcony, or in front of an open window for several hours a day, bringing them in at night. After several days of this half-in and half-out procedure, they will be ready to be planted out in their permanent home.

Even nurseries do not achieve 100 percent perfection with their pot-grown plants so, if you are buying plants, make your selection carefully. Choose plants that are evenly colored – discoloring is a sign of weakness and poor health – and free from insects. Whitefly, for example, is a persistent predator, and you can do without introducing it to your garden or home on an imported plant. Also, look for signs of vigorous growth; plants with strong stems and several branches will continue to perform well.

If you are uncertain about the fragrance of a plant, and are not sure you want to include it in your selection, brush the leaves lightly with your hand to release the scent. Do not resort to the more brutal tactic of pinching a leaf, which can cause bruising.

Finally, make sure all the plants you buy are clearly labeled before you leave the garden center or nursery. Several herbs have similar leaves, and if you are not yet familiar with the individual aromas, confusion can quite easily arise.

Setting plants out in the garden gives them something of a culture shock so it is important to do it at the right time of day. Hot sun causes the plants to wilt so much they may take days to recover, so transplant them on a cloudy day or, in a hot spell, early in the morning or late in the afternoon. Dig holes for the incoming plants and water them well so the plants immediately have one of their main requirements for healthy growth – a supply of moisture.

If you are using regular pots and not peat pots, take care to keep intact the maximum amount of soil around the roots of each plant. To do this, tip the pot upside down to release the roots and soil and hold it in your hand. If the roots look bunched up together, gently ease them out at the sides, still keeping soil around them. Set each plant in its hole, with the top of the roots only just below the level of the ground. Press a little soil around the roots and give them a light sprinkling of water. Now fill the hole with more soil, pack it around the plant so the roots can get a good hold, and water again. Continue to water the plants at frequent intervals until new leaves appear. This indicates that the roots have become established, and all is well.

To plant herbs in containers, place a layer of broken crockery (such as pieces of broken flower pots) in the bottom and fill the vessel to within 1 in/2.5 cm of the rim with a good-quality potting soil. Then plant the herbs in the way described above.

DIVIDING PLANTS

RIGHT: To divide a clump of chives, you can remove small, well-rooted pieces from the side to form new plants.

RIGHT: Another way is to tease the clump apart and make several or many new plants.

FAR RIGHT: Set out the new plants about 1 ft/30 cm apart to grow into mature clumps.

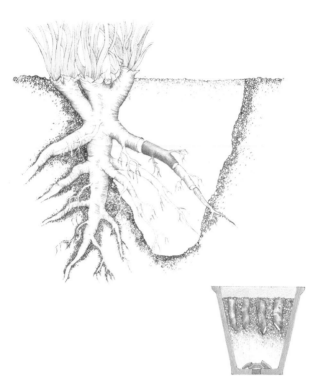

L E F T : Herbaceous perennials can be increased by taking root cuttings. Divide thick roots into 3 in/7 cm lengths. Plant them, straight side up, level with the soil surface and cover with sand. Leave them in a closed frame for the winter.

A B O V E : To layer a shoot, select one close to the soil, making a slanting cut halfway through the underside of a stem opposite a bud or leaf joint on the upper side. Keep the cut open with a matchstick or a small stone, and anchor the layer in good soil with a hooked wire so that the cut faces the soil. Bend the tip upward. As soon as the layer is well rooted, cut it away from the parent stem.

PROPAGATION

Woody perennial herbs and shrubs can be grown from layered shoots and cuttings, a far quicker method than growing from seed.

Select leggy shoots of sage and, while they are still attached to the plant, make a few nicks at intervals along their length, using a sharp knife. Place them along the ground and peg at intervals, using staples of bent wire. Lightly cover the shoots with soil, and they will produce roots along their length. You can then cut the shoots away from the parent plant, and, if you wish, transplant each small, rooted plant to another site or give them to friends.

Layering roots or, more accurately, rhizomes of mint at the end of summer is a similar technique, and one that enables you to enjoy fresh young leaves of mint throughout the winter. Lift one root at the end of summer and cut a few of the rhizomes into short lengths, say about 6 in/15 cm. Lay them in a box of soil, cover lightly with more soil, and bring them indoors. They will soon send out shoots and provide new leaf growth, far more aromatic than the toughened leaves on the plant at the end of the season.

Spring and early summer is the time to take cuttings of woody herbs such as thyme and rosemary. Tear off about 2 in/5 cm of new young growth to leave a "heel"; this gives far more successful results than cutting off the shoot with pruners. Insert the cuttings around the edge of a pot containing sandy soil, and press the growing medium firmly around the stems. Leave the cuttings to root, and keep them indoors or under glass during the first winter. They can be planted out during the following spring.

1 A healthy, well-developed plant can yield several cuttings. Use your discretion and do not cut it back too hard, or you will weaken the plant.

2 To take a cutting, make a slanting cut just under a leaf joint, about 4 in/10 cm from the tip. Strip off the lower leaves and stipules.

3 Dip the ends of each cutting in a hormone rooting compound and insert them around the rim of a pot of gritty soil. Water lightly.

CARE AND MAINTENANCE

Herbs are fairly undemanding once they are established in the garden or in containers. The main task is to keep the area free of weeds, which can suffocate young plants. Harvesting the leaves and pinching out flowering shoots encourages more bushy growth.

Since most herbs originate from dry climates they do not need – and most do not want – rigorous watering, and they can survive long dry spells. However, you will soon see when they appear to be losing their freshness and are in need of a gentle soaking.

Perennial herbs such as thyme and sage tend to become woody, and the plants benefit from cutting back at the end of the season. Even so, there comes a time when they will not retain or regain their original compact shape, and therefore it is best to renew plants every few years.

Caring for plants in a container garden carries rather more responsibility, since they do not have their roots in the soil with all its natural ingredients to feed them. Water plants daily in a dry spell, and add an organic fertilizer at least every two weeks so they have adequate nourishment. If you are leaving shrubby plants such as bay to overwinter outdoors, protect the roots from frost by wrapping the whole container in burlap. It may not be aesthetically pleasing, but is a necessary and effective protection.

Keep indoor herb plants in the sunniest spot you can find. In an ideal world, they like about five hours of sunlight or 10 hours of strong artificial light a day. Turn the pots from time to time so the herbs do not grow unevenly toward the light, and inspect them regularly for insect attack. If you find insects on the plants, wash the leaves in soapy water or spray with an organic pesticide. Do not use chemical preparations on herbs you are just about to eat.

HARVESTING

Harvesting your herbs will be a continuing process, as you pick leaves to use in the kitchen. Harvesting for drying, however, needs both care and careful timing. In general, it is best to gather herbs for keeping just before the plant comes into flower, when the volatile oils, and therefore the fragrance, are at their strongest. Gather them on a dry day after the morning dew has dried off, and before the sun is at its height, when it draws the aroma from the leaves.

To dry the herbs you can hang them in bunches, each type separately, or spread them on racks. A piece of muslin stretched over a wooden frame is the traditional way; a shallow basket or baking trays are the modern equivalents.

Hang the bunches or place the trays in a warm, airy place, such as above a radiator, where they will take from two to eight days to dry. The ideal temperature to dry the herbs quickly is 70°–80°F/21°–27°C. If this is not feasible, you might prefer to dry them in the oven at its lowest setting, with the door left open to allow the moisture to escape. They will take an hour or so. Another method is to spread herb leaves out on paper towels and dry them in the microwave on high for up to two minutes. Whichever method you choose, the herbs will be ready when they feel crisp and papery.

RIGHT : A trio of sturdy pots closely planted with thyme make an attractive feature on a pathway or the corner of a terrace.

RIGHT : A small "parsley pot" with holes at intervals around its circumference makes an attractive planter for a windowsill. This one is planted with bay, mint and parsley.

When they are dry, you can store the leaves in bunches hanging in a closet to use later in cooking, pot pourri, and decorations. Or crumble them lightly in your fingers, and store in airtight jars away from the light. Note, however, that bay leaves give best results stored whole.

Harvest seeds for drying as soon as they start to ripen on the plant. Hang them in bunches, the seed-heads protected by a paper bag to collect falling seed, and hang them in a warm, airy place for up to two weeks. Rub off the seed, and store it in airtight containers away from strong light.

Freezing is another highly successful means of storing herb leaves. Simply freeze stems of parsley, basil, mint, thyme, and others in a plastic bag, and crumble them as you need them to cook with. Or – the "freshest" way of all – chop the herbs finely, pack them into ice-cube trays, fill with water, and freeze. Once frozen, turn out the cubes and store in a plastic bag. Thaw them in a strainer as required, and the herbs will emerge as good as fresh.

As a decorative variation on a theme, freeze bright blue borage flowers and a few mint leaves in ice cubes and add them to summer drinks. Take the drinks in your herb garden on a summer's evening, and your herb growing will have come full circle.

A B O V E : Gather herbs for drying early in the season, and early in the day, when the volatile oils, and therefore the fragrance, are at their strongest.

L E F T : Hang herbs to dry in a room corner or a north-facing window. Do not hang them in strong sunlight, which fades the herbs and draws out the aroma.

CHAPTER 2

Using Herbs

*W*ith a few pots of herbs on a windowsill, a tub of contrasting herbs on a balcony, or a small plot devoted to a careful selection of aromatic plants, you have fragrance at your fingertips – fragrance you can use in cooking, in health-maintaining preparations, cosmetics, and decorations around the home.

A collection of herbs to use as condiments is the single most beneficial weapon in a cook's armory, the one that can transform everyday dishes into master-pieces. Fresh, dried, or frozen, herbs can bring out the flavor of bland foods such as chicken and eggs; they can offset the richness of fatty meats like goose, duck, and pork, and the oiliness of fish such as mackerel. In marinades and casseroles they can impregnate meat and fish with subtle flavors and help in the tenderizing process, while in desserts they can both sweeten and flavor sauces and creams, turning simple puddings into sophisticated dishes. Herbs can be blended with butter to spread in sandwiches or drizzle over broiled chops and steaks; they can be infused in oils and vinegars for use in cooking and salad dressings; they can be used as versatile garnishes for both sweet and savory dishes of all kinds.

A tisane of a single herb or a subtle blend can, according to which herbs are used, be a stimulating and refreshing or a relaxing and soporific drink, and many can be a positive aid to digestion. Similar infusions can be used on the skin and for the hair; and herbs can be blended with unperfumed cold cream and other products to make naturally aromatic cosmetics.

Dried herbs have a fragrant part to play in pot pourri, the medley of floral scents that was widely used in the great houses of the Elizabethan era, while both fresh and dried herbs can be used in flower arrangements, in decorative wreaths and rings, and in other ways to enhance the home.

HERBS IN COOKING

Sometimes it is a single herb that does most to complement a dish: basil with tomato and mozzarella salad; summer savory with the first-picked young green beans; a sprig of rosemary with roast lamb; sage and onion stuffing with pork; a bay leaf infused in a creamy custard. At other times a partnership of herbs is traditional, as with parsley and thyme stuffing to bring out the flavor in chicken; tarragon and chervil in bearnaise sauce to serve with beef; parsley and chives in potato salad; and caraway and coriander seeds in satay sauce to serve with Oriental dishes.

For robust country dishes, soups, and stews, a blend of several herbs is often best, with no single one pre-dominating. In such cases, when three or four herbs are used in unison they can be made into a fresh or dried bouquet garni. This can consist of a sprig or two of fresh parsley and thyme, a bay leaf, and perhaps a twist of thinly pared orange rind, the bunch tied with twine and added to the dish to impart its mixed flavors slowly and surely, and then removed. Or the bouquet garni can be made of a teaspoon or so of dried herbs – parsley, thyme, oregano, and rosemary, perhaps – or the classic French blend of *fines herbes* used for chicken and fish dishes, consisting of chervil, chives, parsley, and tarragon. In this way the dried herbs are tied into a piece of fine scalded muslin or, in those commercially available, sealed into perforated sachets, like tea bags.

You might want to experiment with a blend of herbs when making an omelet, a cheese dish, tea bread, or savory biscuits/crackers or – a host of dishes for which a bouquet garni would be inappropriate. In such cases, when the herbs are to be an integral part of the dish, it is a good idea to blend a pinch or two of each in a saucer, and then test the combined aroma before committing it to the dish.

Making herb oils and vinegars is a good way to have a range of herbal flavors on hand: basil oil to cook ratatouille, fennel oil to brush on fish, tarragon oil or vinegar to marinate chicken, lemon thyme vinegar for a salad dressing, and so on.

To make herb oil, choose a good-quality sunflower, safflower, corn or olive oil and pour it into a screw-topped bottle or jar. To every 1¼ cups/300 ml of oil add 2 tablespoons/30 ml crushed fresh herb leaves or 1 tablespoon/15 ml crushed seeds. You can use a single fragrance or, if you prefer, a blend of two or more herbs. Add 1 tablespoon/15 ml of wine vinegar or cider vinegar and 4 or 5 black peppercorns. Close the bottle or jar, shake it vigorously, and leave it in a

OPPOSITE:
Decorative pats and blocks of herb butter are delicious as sandwich fillings, or to drizzle over broiled steak, chops and fish.

BELOW: Pack a jar with fresh leaves of French tarragon and fill it with vinegar to make a pleasantly aromatic and versatile condiment.

sunny place for two weeks, shaking it once or twice a day. At the end of this time strain off the herbs – using a filter paper for herb seeds – and press them firmly against the strainer to extract all the flavor. Repeat the process with more fresh herbs. After the second infusion, pour the flavored oil into a clean bottle and add a sprig or two of fresh herbs for decoration. Close the bottle and label it clearly with the type of oil and herbs used in the preparation.

Herb vinegar is made in a similar way. Choose distilled white vinegar, white wine vinegar, or cider vinegar. You will need 1 oz/25 g crushed fresh herb leaves or 1 tablespoon/15 ml crushed seeds to each 1¼ cups/300 ml vinegar. Pack the leaves into a bottle or jar, pour on the vinegar, and add a few black peppercorns. Close the vessel, shake it well, and set it aside in a sunny place for 10 days, shaking it daily. Strain off the herbs and repeat the process once more. Pour the flavored vinegar into a clean bottle, cover, and label it.

To make garlic oil or vinegar, immerse several peeled and chopped cloves of garlic in good-quality oil or vinegar, leave for several days and strain. Garlic oil is especially good in salads and for stir-fried dishes.

HERB TEAS

In Victorian times, ladies were inclined to sip a cup of reviving herb tea as a cure for all kinds of perceived discomforts and illnesses. Today the habit of drinking herbal teas, whether or not as an aid to health disorders, is gaining popularity once again, particularly among those who wish to avoid the stimulants in tea and coffee. These tisanes are easy to make and, with a few herbs to ring the changes, offer a variety unequaled by any other type of beverage.

You can make the tisane in a cup for a single serving, in a teapot kept especially for the purpose – glass ones are particularly attractive – or in an enamel pot. Do not use metal containers.

For each cup of tea, you need 1 teaspoon/5 ml dried herbs or lightly crushed herb seeds, or 1 tablespoon/15 ml fresh herbs. Pour the boiling water over the herb, stir well, and leave it to infuse for five to 10 minutes. Strain it, add a little honey if you like, and drink the tisane hot or cold. A twist of lemon or orange added to the cup or glass can help bring out the herb's subtle flavor.

When you wish to extract the beneficial elements from plant roots, the process – though still an infusion – is known as a decoction. English mallow root decoction, for instance, was taken for sore throats in the days when self-help medicines were all that was available. To make a decoction, you need 1 oz/25 g of the root to each 1¼ cups/300 ml of water. Put the chopped root in a heatproof glass or enamel pan – do not use a metal one – and bring to a boil. Simmer for 15 minutes, then strain.

Lemon verbena tea for sleeplessness, dill tisane for flatulence, borage tea for coughs, and sage tea – one of the most widespread of folkloric medicines – for sore throats and other winter ills, yarrow tea applied to cuts and bruises, and hyssop tea as a gargle: you will see the range of medicinal uses to which these tisanes were put as you read through the Directory. In these days of advanced medical knowledge you may prefer to drink the tisanes simply because they are, at their most basic, pleasant and soothing beverages. We make no claims for their medicinal properties.

Many herbal oils and vinegars, tisanes and decoctions have cosmetic uses, too, their supposed properties handed down from generations past. Herbal oils can be used for massage in the aromatherapy way – though homemade ones contain very little of the essential plant oil – while herbal vinegars can be added to the rinsing water after shampooing the hair or washing clothes. Both oils and vinegars can be added to bath

BELOW : Herbal teas, known as tisanes, were popular in Victorian times and are now enjoying a comeback. According to type, they can be refreshing, soothing or stimulating.

RIGHT : Herbs and flowers steeped in natural oils, vinegar or water make gentle cosmetics, hair and bath preparations with an air of pampered luxury.

OPPOSITE : A harvest of herbs for drying, for cooking and for using in cosmetics makes a delightful still-life group in a kitchen alcove.

water, and tisanes may be used on the hair and skin. Chamomile, marigold, and rosemary tea as hair rinse, southernwood tea to combat dandruff, chervil or elderflower tea as a skin freshener – there is a long list of cosmetic uses for herbal infusions.

DECORATING WITH HERBS

Even if they had no culinary, medicinal, or cosmetic applications, many herbs would be worth growing for their decorative and aromatic properties alone. Bunches of tansy and marjoram flowers hanging in a corner, a pot of fresh herb leaves – lemon balm, sweet cicely, fennel, and sage, perhaps – on the kitchen table, evergreen herbs bound to a twig ring on a wall, and a dish of fragrant pot pourri to scent a living room or bedroom: herbs have a great deal to offer in terms of good looks and pleasing aroma.

Pot pourri is one of the most delightful means of preserving herbs, and one that can be decorative as well as aromatic. Harvest herb flowers and leaves as for drying – that is, on a dry day and when the dew has evaporated – and hang them or spread them out to dry; see Chapter 1, under the heading *Harvesting*, for details. Choose some flowers for their appearance – borage, sage, chamomile, carnations, and marigolds, say – and others, such as lavender, for their perfume. Gather leaves as much for their shape and color as for their aroma. Small scented geranium leaves, for instance, are a pretty addition to any mixture.

As the materials dry, sort them for color and store accordingly in wide-necked airtight jars. You might like to make one golden pot pourri blend with a hint of blue for contrast, one romantically based on deep pinks, reds, and blues, and one, a refreshing contrast, of yellow and white.

When the blend of dried materials is complete, add the spices, fixative, and oils that will draw the various aromas together and stabilize the scent. To every 5 cups of flowers, petals, and leaves allow 1 tablespoon/ 15 ml of ground spices, such as cinnamon or ginger, and add a pinch of grated nutmeg and ground cloves. Add 2½ tablespoons/40 ml of the fixative, ground orris root powder, and 3 drops of essential oil, both of which you can buy in some drugstores and health food stores. The oil may be attar of roses, rosemary, neroli, or lemon, for instance, or even a special pot pourri blend of different fragrances.

Stir all the ingredients together, close the jar, and leave it for eight to 10 weeks, shaking or stirring it almost daily. When the aromas have blended and the spices no longer smell raw, display the pot pourri in decorative bowls, baskets, a pretty cup and saucer, in dainty sachets and bags, what you will. It is a delightful way to bring your herb garden indoors and capture the mingled scents of a summer evening.

Herb Directory

Achillea millefolium
YARROW

Bunches of yarrow hanging to dry in a warm airy room; the flat white flowerheads providing highlights in a dried flower arrangement in a summer fireplace; a few of the pungent leaves added sparingly to a mixed green salad . . .

Common yarrow, a hardy perennial and native to Europe, grows as a rampant weed in fields and hedgerows, where it can vary from a low, creeping form to a tough plant up to 24 in/60 cm high. It has flat heads of minute five-petaled white flowers. Other forms (*A. millefolium v. rosea* and *A. filipendulina*, respectively) have pink-and-cream or bright yellow flowers.

HISTORY

The plant's generic name is believed to derive from the Greek hero Achilles, who is said to have used it to heal his soldiers' wounds during the Trojan War. Accordingly, it has been called *herba militaris*, the military herb, knight's milfoil, bloodwort and staunchweed.

CHARACTERISTICS

The leaves are about 4 in/10 cm long, dark green, downy and feathery, and the stems are pale green, rough and angular. The plant flowers from early summer to late autumn.

GROWING TIPS

The plant thrives in full sun but will tolerate shade. It is easily grown in any type of soil, even in poor soil, and is increased by dividing the roots.

HOW TO USE

Fresh leaves may be used in salads. They have a slightly pungent taste and are very aromatic.

In self-help medicine, fresh leaves were applied to wounds as an aid to healing. An infusion of fresh or dried leaves may be used to apply to minor cuts and grazes, and a decoction may be used to wash the hair; it was thought to prevent baldness. It can also be helpful as an astringent for greasy skin.

YARROW & CHAMOMILE LOTION

Ingredients

1 tbsp dried yarrow flowers
1 tbsp dried chamomile flowers
1 cup boiling water

Excellent for oily skins

Preparation

- Place the flowers in a bowl, pour the water over, stir once, then cover and leave in a warm place for 30 minutes.
- Stir again, then strain off the liquid.
- Pour into bottles with glass stoppers or screw caps.

OPPOSITE: Bathed in warm sunlight, this closely packed herb border illustrates some of the visual contrasts you can achieve with aromatic and herbaceous plants.

BELOW LEFT: In its natural habitat, yarrow stands out like so many snowflakes against the grassy background.

BELOW: With its umbel-like clusters of minute white flowers and ladderlike leaves, yarrow is an attractive addition to an herbaceous border.

R I G H T : Cloves of garlic wrapped in their papery sheaths and broken away from the bulb represent untold depths of flavor packed into such small and insignificant-looking units.

Allium sativum
GARLIC

Golden garlic-fried croûtons garnishing a creamy vegetable soup; a clove of garlic rubbed around a salad bowl to impart just a hint of the flavor; slivers of the bulb tucked into slits of lamb for broiling or roasting . . .

A member of the onion family, the garlic bulb is an indispensable flavoring in cooking and is widely used throughout southern Europe, the Middle East, the Far East, Africa, the West Indies, Mexico, and North and South America. A native of Asia, it is easily grown and widely cultivated in warm climates throughout the world. It can be grown successfully in northern Europe and in North America, but in cooler conditions the bulb never reaches its maximum flavor potential.

HISTORY

Garlic has been used medicinally and as a flavoring for at least 5,000 years, and has been cultivated in the Mediterranean region since the time of the ancient Egyptians. The Anglo-Saxons grew it, too, and gave it its name: *gar*, a lance, and *leac*, a leek. Roman soldiers ate it as a stimulant, and ancient mariners always took it as a part of their ships' stores.

CHARACTERISTICS

The straight, rigid stem, topped by a spherical pink or white flowerhead, grows to a height of 24 in/60 cm. Each bulb is made up of several cloves, which may have white, pink, or purple skin, encased in a paper-like sheath. The size, number, and flavor of the cloves vary considerably according to the variety and the climate; garlic may be highly pungent or almost sweet. The bright green leaves are long, straight, slender, and round, like those of chives.

GROWING TIPS

Garlic grows best in well-drained soil in a sunny position. Cloves are planted in the autumn or in early spring to mature in summer. They should be planted 1 in/

2.5 cm deep and up to 8 in/20 cm apart, and should be given a good start with the application of a general fertilizer to the soil.

It is said that if garlic is planted beneath a peach tree it will prevent leafcurl, and that it can ward off aphids and blackspot on roses.

HOW TO USE

Garlic cloves may be finely chopped or crushed with a garlic press and used to complement the flavor of meat, fish, vegetables, salad dressings, sauces, and egg dishes. In southern Europe, sauces such as *aioli* (garlic mayonnaise) and *skordalia* are made from raw garlic, and in one French dish chicken is cooked surrounded by whole cloves of garlic and salt. Some people find

the aftertaste of garlic offensive on the breath; chewing fennel seeds can alleviate this problem.

Whole cloves, peeled, may be preserved in jars filled with olive oil; the flavored oil may then be used as a salad dressing.

Garlic has positive health-giving properties. It may be used as an antiseptic; to tone up the digestive system; to reduce blood pressure; and to clear catarrh and bronchitis. It has also been used as a diuretic and as a combatant to diseases such as typhoid.

GARLIC MASH

Ingredients
Serves 6
3 heads of garlic (about 35 cloves)
¼ lb butter
3 tbsp flour
¼ tsp nutmeg
¼ tsp English mustard
1 cup boiling milk
salt and pepper
2 lb floury potatoes
3 tbsp light cream

Garlic Mash is particularly good with sausages, steak, and roast chicken, or as a nest for baked eggs.

Preparation
● Separate the garlic cloves and blanch them in boiling water for 1 minute; drain and peel. Then cook over a low heat, covered, in half the butter for about 20 minutes until tender.
● Blend in the flour, nutmeg and mustard, and stir for several minutes without browning. Remove from the heat and stir in the boiling milk. Season with salt and pepper to taste.
● Return to the heat and simmer for 5 minutes. Sieve or blend to a smooth purée. Return to the pan and simmer for 2 more minutes.
● Peel the potatoes and cut into small chunks. Boil for 15 minutes or until just tender and drain. Mash with the remaining butter.
● Beat in the reheated garlic purée followed by the cream, a spoonful at a time. The final mixture should not be too runny. Check for seasoning and serve immediately.

Allium schoenoprasum
CHIVES

Snipped chives mingling with sour cream in a dressing for baked potatoes; chive leaves and carrot "flowers" making a decorative garnish on a vegetable pâté; pats of chive butter drizzling over charcoal-grilled steaks . . .

Chives, a member of the onion family and grown from bulbs, are native to northern Europe, where they may sometimes be found growing wild. They also thrive in temperate regions of North America. The leaves have a delicate, onionlike flavor and are widely used in cooking, particularly in egg and cheese dishes, in salads, and as a garnish. If protected under a cloche, they can be harvested for nine months of the year. Chives are included in the *fines herbes* mixture used in French cookery.

HISTORY

In the Middle Ages, chives were known as "rush-leek," from the Greek *schoinos*, rush, and *prason*, a leek. They were used in antiquity, and have been cultivated since the sixteenth century.

CHARACTERISTICS

Chives grow in clumps, with their round, hollow, grasslike leaves reaching a height of 9 in/23 cm. Some varieties, *A. sibiricum* for example, may be 15 in/38 cm tall. The stems are firm, straight, smooth and, like the leaves, bright dark green. The flowers, which bloom for two months in midsummer, form round, deep-mauve or pink heads and are attractive used as a garnish.

GROWING TIPS

Chives flourish in a moist, well-drained soil and like partial shade, though they can tolerate full sun. Seed may be sown in late spring or late summer, or the plants may be increased by dividing the clumps in mid-spring. Chives grow particularly well in pots, and are a good choice for a kitchen windowsill garden.

HOW TO USE

Snipped chives – for it is easier to cut them with scissors than chop them with a knife – give a hint of onion flavor in many dishes, from scrambled egg to cheese soufflé. They are good sprinkled on green and tomato salads, on soups, in cream cheese sandwiches, and on baked potatoes with sour cream dressing. Chive butter, made by beating snipped chives and lemon juice into softened butter, is good with broiled chops and steak.

The leaves are slightly antiseptic, and were used to relieve rheumatism.

OPPOSITE ABOVE: A single ram-rod straight stem of flowering chives and two round, hollow leaves illustrate the statuesque nature of the plant.

OPPOSITE BELOW: A thick cluster of chives topped by their pinky-mauve flower domes is one of the prettiest and most colorful features of a herb garden.

CHICKEN, CHEESE & CHIVE TERRINE

Ingredients
Serves 8
12 oz boneless chicken breast
6 tbsp brandy
1 clove garlic, crushed
1 tbsp chopped fresh parsley
12 oz boneless chicken thighs
1½ lb stewing pork
3 slices bacon
7 oz cream cheese
½ cup heavy cream
2 eggs
grated rind of ½ lemon
1 tbsp chopped fresh chives
salt and freshly ground black pepper
Oven temperature: 400°F.

Preparation
• Marinate the chicken breasts in the brandy, garlic, and half the parsley for 2 minutes.
• Preheat the oven. Grind the chicken thighs, pork, and bacon together. Blend with the cream cheese, cream, beaten eggs, and lemon rind. Add the parsley, chives, and the marinade drained from the chicken. Season well.
• Put a third of the chicken forcemeat into a lightly oiled 2-qt loaf pan or terrine dish. Top with half the chicken breasts, then another layer of forcemeat, then the rest of the chicken breasts and, finally, the remaining forcemeat.
• Cover and bake in a roasting pan of water for approximately 1½-2 hours.
• Cool, then press with a weight and refrigerate for at least 24 hours.
• To garnish, invert the terrine onto a wire cooling rack. Spoon over some cool, half-set aspic jelly to form a glaze. Decorate the surface of the terrine with chive stems, red pepper and egg shapes, then coat with another layer of aspic.

CHARACTERISTICS

The woody stems are tough, angular and have many branches, giving the plant, which grows to a height of 5 ft/1.5 m, its bushy, spreading characteristic. The long, pointed-oval and pale green leaves are about 4 in/10 cm long and ½ in/12 mm wide. The flowers, which grow in clusters along the stem, are pale purple and bloom in late summer.

GROWING TIPS

A perennial, deciduous shrub, lemon verbena is hardy to a temperature of 40°F/4°C. This means that in cool climates it needs protection in winter. It may be grown from seed, or from soft cuttings taken in July and grown in sandy soil under cover. The bush should be pruned in spring to contain its growth and remove dead wood.

HOW TO USE

The strong citrus aroma is used to flavor stuffings for meat, poultry, and fish, in fish dishes and sauces, fruit salads, poached fruit, soft drinks, and cream desserts. The herb may be substituted for lemongrass in southeast Asian dishes.

Fresh or dried leaves may be used medicinally, as a mild sedative and as a help for indigestion and flatulence, or may be infused to make a mild skin toner and skin freshener.

The dried leaves are an invaluable ingredient in pot pourri, particularly when used to scent bed linen or in an herbal sleep pillow.

Aloysia triphylla
LEMON VERBENA

ABOVE: The long, pointed oval leaves of lemon verbena are packed with a subtle citruslike aroma.

ABOVE RIGHT: Towering high above other herbs and flowering plants, lemon verbena makes a striking impact in any herb garden.

Baked trout made all the more aromatic with a lemon verbena stuffing; pears poached in a syrup flavored with the lemony herb; a green and gold pot pourri blended with the sharp, tangy fragrance of the leaves . . .

One of the most delightful of scented plants, lemon verbena has a strong citrus aroma that is at its most powerful in the early evening. A native of South America, it thrives best in hot climates, where it will grow up to 5 ft/1.5 m tall and almost as wide. It is, therefore, a good choice as a back-of-the-bed plant in sunny borders.

HISTORY

The plant was brought to Europe by the Spaniards, and was used as a source of fragrant oil for perfume.

Althaea officinalis
ENGLISH MALLOW

The young, bright green shoots shredded and added to mixed salads, or chopped over avocado salad; the roots, lightly boiled, fried in sizzling butter and garnished with chopped coriander . . .

A member of the hollyhock family, English mallow has small, attractive flowers carried without stems. It is grown throughout Europe, in Australia, Asia, and eastern North America. The mucilage, which comprises about 30 percent of the roots, stems, and leaves, was used to make the confection known as marshmallow, but now substitutes are used commercially.

HISTORY

The plant's medicinal properties have been recognized since ancient times. Mallow features in a second-century BC herbal, and was illustrated in another from the sixth century AD.

CHARACTERISTICS

The plant grows to a height of up to 4 ft/1.2 m, with a spread of 18 in/45 cm. The long, tapering root is cream colored and fleshy, somewhat resembling a parsnip, and the bright green leaves are heart shaped and irregularly toothed, with pronounced veins in a yellowish green and a downy coating on both sides. The five-petaled flowers are saucer shaped, white or pink, and about 1½ in/4 cm across. They bloom in late summer. The plant has no fragrance.

GROWING TIPS

English mallow likes it damp, and may be found growing wild on marshland. A perennial, it can be grown from seed sown outdoors in spring, or increased by dividing the roots in autumn. It is important to keep the plants moist, especially during a dry summer.

HOW TO USE

The young leaves and shoots may be shredded and added to salads and soups; the roots may be parboiled, then fried in butter.

The plant was used in self-help medicine for sprains, bruises, and muscular pain. An infusion of the dried root was used to treat sore throats and ulcers, while an infusion of flowers was used as a mouthwash.

ABOVE: With its pale sugar-almond pink flowers and downy leaves, English mallow is attractive enough to use in summer flower arrangements.

LEFT: In the damp conditions that it favors, English mallow will grow to a height of 4 ft/1.2 m.

ABOVE: Dill leaves, soft, feathery and densely packed, are perfect candidates for drying, when they are known as dill weed.

Anethum graveolens
DILL

Fresh dill leaves – known as dill weed – in a sauce to serve with oven-baked bream; chopped dill stirred into yogurt as a dressing for cucumber; dill seed as a pickling spice for gherkins . . .

The plant originates from southern Europe and western Asia, and its use is recorded far back in time. As with so many umbellifers, this hardy annual yields two separate culinary components, its seeds and its feathery leaves, which are, somewhat ambiguously, known as dill weed.

HISTORY

The herb was used medicinally by doctors in both ancient Egypt and Rome; indeed, it was the Romans who introduced it to northern Europe. After centuries in obscurity, it surfaced again in medieval times, when its use was widespread, particularly in Scandinavian countries like Norway and Sweden.

CHARACTERISTICS

Dill grows to a height of 2½ ft/75 cm, with a spread of 12 in/30 cm. The green stem, which is hollow and smooth, branches out at the top and carries large flat umbellifers of bright yellow flowers that bloom in midsummer. The leaves are ultra-fine, feathery, and dark green, and have a taste similar to that of parsley. The flat, oval seeds are parchment colored, and have a rather bitter flavor.

GROWING TIPS

The plant is easy to grow from seed sown in late spring or early summer. It favors poor, well-drained soil and a sunny position and, since it does not transplant well, should be sown where it is to grow. If the plant is sited close to fennel, cross pollination is possible.

HOW TO USE

The fresh leaves are used in salads, fish dishes, and sauces to serve with fish. In Germany and eastern Europe it is used in pickles, as a preservative for sour cabbage (sauerkraut) and small cucumbers, known as dill pickles. The seeds produce an oil that is used to make dill water, or gripe water, used to alleviate colic in babies. The seeds are also said to act as a sedative and to ward off hunger.

SOUSED HERRINGS WITH SOUR CREAM

Ingredients
Serves 6
6 fresh herring fillets
1 large Spanish onion, sliced
6 bay leaves
18 whole black peppercorns
1 ¼ cups red wine vinegar mixed with water
1 ¼ cups sour cream
fresh dill, chopped
Oven temperature: 325°F.

Preparation
● Preheat the oven. Wash the herring fillets and pat them dry with paper towels.
● Place some of the thinly sliced onion, a bay leaf, and 3 whole peppercorns on each fish. Roll up the herrings with the tail end away from you. Place in an ovenproof dish and cover with the vinegar and water mixture.
● Place in a moderate oven until the herrings are cooked – about 20 minutes. Let the fish cool in the liquid for several hours or overnight.
● Serve cold with a spoonful of sour cream garnished with chopped dill.

ABOVE: The starlike clusters of yellowish green flowers carried on long stems makes dill a dramatic plant, especially in the sunlight.

Angelica archangelica
ANGELICA

Chopped angelica leaves in a court bouillon for salmon and trout; young shoots as a flavoring for rhubarb compote; candied shoots as a sweetmeat and decoration for cakes and desserts . . .

A giant member of the parsley family, angelica grows up to 5 ft/1.5 m high, with a spread of about 3 ft/ 90 cm. It is native both to northern Europe and to Syria, and grows wild in many parts of the world, decorating the countryside with its bright green shoots of treelike proportions.

HISTORY

In ancient times the plant was believed to ward off evil spirits, and was used at pagan festivals. Its later association with angels, in its botanical name and in many European languages, is thought to derive from the fact that it came into flower on or around May 8, the feast day of St. Michael the Archangel.

CHARACTERISTICS

The whole plant is pleasantly aromatic. It has large fleshy roots that can weigh up to 3 lb/1.3 kg and thick, sturdy and hollow stems that are purple at the base, shading to bright and light green. The plant reaches a height of 5 ft/1.5 m and the huge leaves, made up of three leaflets, are bright green and finely toothed. The flowers, which appear in mid- to late summer, are small and yellowish green in color, forming umbrella-like clusters.

This is a plant for large borders! Angelica, a perennial that may live for three years, can be grown only from seed planted in good moist soil in late summer and early autumn. The young plants should be thinned out in spring and planted 3 ft/90 cm apart on their permanent site the following autumn. It is likely that plants will not flower until the second summer. When they do, self-sown seeds will almost certainly result. Removing the flowers before they seed will extend the life of the plant.

HOW TO USE

The fleshy stems are candied as cake decorations and sweetmeat. Young shoots may be blanched, chopped, and added to salads, and the leaves used to flavor *court bouillon* for fish, stewed fruits (rhubarb, in particular), and preserves. Oil from the seeds is used as a flavoring in several aperitifs and other alcoholic drinks, including absinthe and gin. It is also used as an aromatic ingredient in pot pourri.

Medicinally, the dried roots may be used as an aid to flatulence, and the leaves, shoots, and seeds to help relieve coughs, colds, and other respiratory disorders. The seeds may also be used as an appetite stimulant and an aid to digestion.

BELOW RIGHT: Silhouetted against a background of low-growing herbs, angelica is one of the most "architectural" plants in the herb garden.

BELOW: Clusters of angelica seedheads, and large fleshy leaves carried on stems which, when candied, make a delicious sweetmeat.

Anthemis nobilis
CHAMOMILE

Chamomile tea as a soothing drink for Peter Rabbit and others with nervous excitement or stomach ailments; a springy, daisy-flowered chamomile lawn . . .

Apple-scented chamomile, a perennial plant of the composite family, is one of the daintiest of herbs. A low-growing type known as Roman chamomile can be grown as an effective ground cover to form a green and white daisy-flowered lawn.

HISTORY

It is said that the ancient Egyptians used chamomile as a cure for ague. Its use was widespread in the Middle Ages, not only in southern Europe, where it originates, but throughout northern Europe, too. It is mentioned as a medicinal herb in both John Gerard's and Nicholas Culpeper's herbals.

CHARACTERISTICS

The plant may grow to a height of 12 in/30 cm. It has shallow, fibrous roots and a green, hairy, branching stem. The leaves are finely cut and feathery, and the flowers, which come in summer, are compact and creamy white with yellow conical centers.

GROWING TIPS

The plant is easily grown from the division of runners, which are planted out in early spring, and from seed; it is also a prolific self-seeder. It prefers a fertile, moist soil in a sunny position, but will cling tenaciously to life in a poor, well-drained soil. There is a nonflowering variety, Treneague, which some people prefer to use for lawns.

HOW TO USE

What the plant lacks in culinary uses – there are none – it makes up for in other ways. A tisane of the flowers is taken for dyspepsia, flatulence, and other stomach ailments, and used as a mild antiseptic. It can also be taken as an appetite restorer.

An infusion of the dried flowers is used as a rinse for fair hair, as a skin cleanser, and a skin tonic. One species, *A. tinctoria*, is used as an orange-brown dye.

A B O V E : Shaggy stems of chamomile, with their small, insignificant leaves, are topped by delicate, daisylike cream flowers.

L E F T : A dense patch of chamomile is seen growing among other herbs, the dainty flowers all turned to face the sun.

CHAMOMILE CLEANSING MILK

Ingredients
3 tbsp chamomile flowers
1¼ cups warm milk

As this lotion is based on milk, it must be kept in a cool place and will not last for more than 2 or 3 days. It is excellent for oily skins.

Preparation
● Leave the flowers to infuse in the warm milk until the milk smells strongly of chamomile. As it is important that a skin should not form on the milk, and essential that the milk should not be allowed to boil, the best way of keeping the infusion warm is to use a bowl placed over a saucepan of hot water off the heat.
● Stir the milk gently from time to time so as not to break up the flowers.
● Strain the scented milk into a screw-topped bottle or jar.

Anthriscus cerefolium
CHERVIL

Tiny sprigs of garden-fresh chervil added to béchamel sauce as an accompaniment to fish; the curled and lacy leaves used as a garnish for cheese or chicken dishes; the chopped fresh leaves added to a fluffy omelet on the point of serving . . .

Chervil, together with chives, parsley, and tarragon, is one of the *fines herbes* mixture used in French cooking, particularly to flavor omelets. It is also one of the herbs used in *ravigote* sauces, and is often blended with tarragon to flavor béchamel and other creamy sauces. It is a hardy annual, one that is easy to grow but that quickly goes to seed.

HISTORY

The plant is a native of the Middle East, southern Russia, and the Caucasus, and was almost certainly introduced to northern Europe by the Romans. It became one of the classic herbs used in French cooking, in which it is considered indispensable.

CHARACTERISTICS

A member of the umbellifer family, chervil is closely related to parsley. It grows to a height of 20 in/50 cm, with a spread of about 8 in/20 cm. It has flat, light green and lacy leaves, which have a slightly aniseed-like aroma and turn reddish brown as the plant matures. It blooms in midsummer, producing flat umbellifers of tiny white flowers.

GROWING TIPS

The plant can be easily grown from seed planted in early spring or late summer in the position where it is to grow; a planter or a window box is ideal. A succession of sowings will produce a harvest well into the winter. It likes a moist, shady position, and should be kept well watered.

HOW TO USE

The leaves quickly lose their flavor and are best added fresh to a dish just before serving. They can be chopped into softened butter to serve with broiled meats or poultry; added as an aromatic garnish to creamy soups; and stirred into egg and cheese dishes. The leaves are also used to flavor white wine vinegar, and may be infused in water as a skin freshener.

ROAST RIB OF BEEF WITH
BEARNAISE SAUCE

Ingredients
Serves 6
4 lb beef rib
salt and freshly ground black pepper
¼ lb unsalted butter
FOR THE BEARNAISE SAUCE
½ lb unsalted butter, cut into cubes
4 shallots, finely chopped
3 tbsp white wine vinegar
2 tbsp fresh tarragon, chopped
½ tsp chopped chervil
pinch of ground black pepper and salt
4 egg yolks
2 tbsp cold water
Oven temperature: 425°F.

Preparation
● Season the rib of beef with salt and pepper, and place in a heavy roasting pan. Melt the butter and cook in a hot oven, browning the meat on both sides. For rare meat, cook for 10 minutes per pound on each side. Remove the meat to a serving platter and keep warm.
● To make the sauce, in a small heavy saucepan melt 1 tbsp butter. Add the shallots. Cook slowly for about 10 minutes, then add the vinegar, half the tarragon and chervil, and salt and pepper to taste. Reduce the sauce to about 2 tsp.
● Cool the mixture and add the egg yolks and cold water. Mix with a whisk over a low heat, or in a double boiler or saucepan. Make sure you amalgamate the eggs with the shallot mixture, but do not cook them or the sauce will be ruined.
● When the egg yolks look thick and creamy, gradually whisk the remaining butter in, making sure the sauce does not separate. If it gets too thick, add a little water.
● When the sauce is finished, add more chopped tarragon and chervil. Keep warm in the double boiler or double saucepan.
● Carve the rib of beef and serve the Bearnaise sauce separately.

ABOVE: Horseradish leaves, which have no aroma and are not used in cooking, are dark green, thick and swordlike.

RIGHT: Horseradish, with its tough dark-green leaves and penetrating roots, will grow in the most inhospitable of places and is often found along the wayside.

Armoracia rusticana
HORSERADISH

The eye-tingling pungency of the ground root blended with cream or yogurt as a sauce for roast beef; the grated root added cautiously to a stuffing for trout; the sauce stirred into piped mashed potato to give it an unmistakeable "bite" . . .

Horseradish sauce, the classic British accompaniment to roast beef, presents this herb at its most pungent, and in its most popular form. The large fleshy roots are strongly aromatic, so much so that they can, like raw onions, make your eyes water as you prepare them. Unusually, for a herb, the large coarse leaves have no aroma and no known uses.

HISTORY

A native of northern Europe, and still found growing wild along roadsides in Britain and North America, horseradish has been used as a flavoring for at least 3,000 years. It was known to the ancient Greeks, and was used in Britain before the time of the Romans. During the Middle Ages, it was used in Germany and Denmark as a condiment, a hot and spicy alternative to mustard.

CHARACTERISTICS

This perennial plant has long, thick, fleshy white roots covered by a rough and hairy brown skin. The leaves, which can be up to 20 in/50 cm long, are deep green and strongly marked with yellow veins. The stem, about 2 ft/60 cm high, carries spikes of tiny white flowers in late spring and early summer.

GROWING TIPS

Horseradish is an avid colonizer of whatever space is available, so restraint is necessary. It is grown by dividing and replanting the root; a piece about 8 in/20 cm long is ideal. It likes a deep, moist soil but will thrive anywhere. To harvest, dig up a piece of the root, wash, and scrape it under water to prevent eye irritation.

HOW TO USE

A food processor is ideal for grating the peeled root. You can store it in vinegar or oil in a screw-topped jar, mix it with cream, sour cream, yogurt, mayonnaise, or cream cheese and dressings for sauces to serve with meat, fish, and potatoes. It is especially good with beef and smoked trout.

POTATO SALAD WITH HORSERADISH

Ingredients
Serves 4
1½ lb new potatoes
⅔ cup sour cream
3 tbsp horseradish, finely grated
pinch of paprika
½ tsp honey
salt and freshly ground black pepper
bunch of spring onions or chives
handful of chopped parsley

Preparation
● Wash the potatoes, but do not peel. Boil in salted water until tender.
● Meanwhile, make the dressing. Combine the sour cream with the horseradish, paprika, and honey. Mix well and season with salt and pepper.
●Trim the spring onions and slit down the stalks so they curl outward; or chop the chives.
● When the potatoes are cooked, slice them while still hot and mix into the dressing with the parsley. Garnish with the onions or chives. Serve immediately, or chill and serve cold.

Artemisia abrotanum
SOUTHERNWOOD

Bunches of southernwood hanging in clothes closets to ward off moths; the dried leaves lightly crumbled in pot pourri or blended with other dried materials in linen sachets .

With the delightful popular names of lad's love and old man, southernwood, a bushy shrub, is grown in many informal gardens and herbaceous borders as a decorative and strongly aromatic plant, which is, however, said to be repellent to bees. The French called it *garde-robe* because they used it in wardrobes to ward off moths.

HISTORY

Dioscorides described the plant as having such fine leaves that it seemed to be "furnished with hair," while in his herbal Culpeper attributes it with the power of curing baldness. He recommended rubbing a paste made of the ashes and salad oil on the head or face to promote hair growth.

RIGHT: A dense patch of southernwood looks so tactile, one longs to bury a hand deep among the fragrant leaves.

CHARACTERISTICS

The plant can grow to a height of 3 ft/90 cm, with a spread of 2 ft/60 cm. The woody stem has many soft, branching shoots covered with strong, feathery, gray-green leaves. The tiny flowers, which appear in late summer, are golden yellow.

BELOW: Southernwood leaves are strong, feathery, and deep gray-green in color. They have a pungent aroma.

GROWING TIPS

The plant likes a rich soil and a sunny position. Take soft cuttings of new shoots in summer and cover until firmly rooted. Protect the plants in harsh winters, and prune them in late spring.

HOW TO USE

The pungent leaves were used in Italy as a flavoring for meat and poultry stuffings, and for cakes, but have few culinary uses now.

Medicinally, the dried plant may be used as an antiseptic and a stimulant. An infusion of the leaves may be used as a hair rinse to combat dandruff, while dried leaves can be used in linen bags to repel insects, and also in pot pourri. A yellow dye can be extracted from the stems.

HOW TO USE

Tarragon has a strong and distinctive flavor, and must be used sparingly, especially as it is usually associated with delicate dishes such as chicken, white fish, creamy sauces, and egg and cheese recipes. Fresh sprigs of the herb are used to flavor vinegar for use in salad dressings and sauces.

L E F T : The leaves of the true French tarragon are long, slender, pointed and a rich dark green.

Artemisia dracunculus TARRAGON

A bottle of glowing-golden tarragon vinegar to use in piquant salad dressings; fresh leaves chopped into classic sauce Bearnaise or the delicately flavored poulet à l'éstragon; light-as-a-feather omelets flavored with fines herbes . . .

A distinction must be made between the true French tarragon or estragon and its Russian counterpart, *A. dracunculoides*, which is much coarser, and has paler leaves and a bitter taste. Contrarily, the latter is easier to grow!

French tarragon has a subtle flavor and is one of the four ingredients of the *fines herbes* mixture. It is one of the great culinary herbs of France, and has a battery of dishes created around it – *poulet à l'étragon* and *oeufs en gelée à l'éstragon*, to name just two.

HISTORY

The plant, a hardy perennial, originates from southern Europe. The reference in its name to a "little dragon" is thought to derive from its folkloric reputation of curing the bites of snakes, serpents, and the like.

CHARACTERISTICS

The plant grows to a height of 3 ft/90 cm, with a spread of up to 18 in/45 cm. The leaves are dark green, long, slender, and pointed, about 3 in/7.5 cm long toward the base of the plant and considerably smaller at the tip of the stems. The flowers are lime green and formed in loose clusters. But the plant neither flowers nor sets seed in a cool climate.

GROWING TIPS

You can grow French tarragon by planting a piece of the rhizome, complete with buds, in spring, or by taking cuttings of young shoots in summer and growing them under a cloche. The plant likes good, well-drained soil, and a sunny, sheltered position.

ORANGE & TARRAGON CHICKEN

Ingredients
Serves 4
1 oz butter
2 tbsp vegetable oil
4 boneless chicken breasts, each about 6 oz
1 large onion, finely chopped
1 cup frozen concentrated orange juice
2/3 cup chicken stock
4 sprigs fresh tarragon or 1 tbsp dried tarragon
1 tbsp cornstarch
2/3 cup sour cream

Preparation
● Heat the butter and oil in a flameproof casserole. Brown the chicken thoroughly on all sides. Put to one side and remove and discard the skin.
● Cook the onion in the casserole for 2–3 minutes. Stir in the orange juice, stock and chopped tarragon. Bring to a boil and return to the casserole. Cover and reduce the heat to a gentle simmer. Cook for 1 hour or until the chicken is tender.
● Blend the cornstarch with 2 tbsp water and stir into the casserole. Bring to a boil, stirring, until the sauce is smooth and thickened. Switch off the heat and stir in the sour cream. Leave to warm through for a few minutes.
● Transfer the chicken breasts onto individual hot dinner plates. Spoon the sauce over the chicken.

LEFT : With their light
blue, star-shaped flowers
and downy leaves,
borage plants make
a focal point in any
herb border.

OPPOSITE : Borage
leaves are used to make a
soothing tisane, while
the flowers are
traditionally used to
decorate summer drinks.

Borago officinalis
BORAGE

Dainty blue borage flowers and young shoots floating in ice-cold summer drinks; the flowers providing a colorful garnish to crisp and crunchy salads; the young leaves lightly boiled and served as an alternative to spinach . . .

The bright blue, star-shaped flowers of borage make it one of the prettiest of herb plants, though the leaves, dark green, downy, and with no fragrance, are un-remarkable. It is a hardy annual, a native of northern Europe, and grows well in the temperate regions of North America.

HISTORY

Borage has, over the centuries, been accredited with legendary powers. Pliny called it *euphrosinum* because it was said to bring happiness and joy wherever it grew. The ancient Greeks and Romans looked to it for comfort and courage, and this belief in its capabilities was revived in the Middle Ages. Gerard, in his *Herball*, quotes, "I, Borage, bring always courage."

CHARACTERISTICS

The leaves have a flavor reminiscent of cucumber. The plant grows to a height of about 18 in/45 cm, with a spread of 12 in/30 cm. It has an untidy, straggling habit, compensated for by the cloud of blue flowers that grow in arched clusters and persist throughout the summer months.

GROWING TIPS

Borage is easy to grow from seed sown outdoors in spring. It likes a sandy soil and sunny position, but will tolerate a heavier soil and partial shade. The plant self-sows seed freely and will, in this way, colonize a large area.

HOW TO USE

Borage flowers and leaves are the traditional decoration for gin-based summer cocktails, and may be set in ice cubes to garnish other drinks. The flowers may be used to garnish salads, and candied for cake decoration.

Borage tisane, an infusion of the leaves, may be taken to ease coughs, and the leaves may be used as a poultice to alleviate muscular strains.

CUCUMBER & AVOCADO WITH BORAGE

Ingredients
Serves 4
2 large cucumbers, about 2 lb total weight
1 small avocado
lemon juice
2 oz unsalted butter
1 shallot, finely chopped
1 small egg, beaten
salt and freshly ground white pepper
1 oz cream cheese, chopped
flowers from 2–3 sprigs borage

Preparation
• Peel the cucumbers and cut each one into 4 equal lengths. Cut out a V-shaped wedge, about a quarter of the diameter of the cucumber, along the length of each piece and scoop out and discard the seeds. Chop the remaining wedges roughly.
• Steam the cucumber lengths for about 12–15 minutes until just tender. Meanwhile, peel, halve, and remove the pit from the avocado. Cut off 8 slices, brush with lemon juice, and reserve for the garnish. Chop the remaining flesh roughly.
• Heat the butter, add the chopped cucumber and shallot, and cook over a moderate heat for 4–5 minutes, stirring occasionally. Remove from the heat and stir in the avocado, egg, and seasoning so the egg scrambles very lightly. Scatter the cheese over, fold through once, then pile the mixture into the cucumber lengths and scatter the borage over the top.
• Serve the filled cucumber immediately with the reserved avocado slices.

Brassica juncea
MUSTARD

The seed germinated indoors and served as a pungent salad; the tiny round seed used as a pickling spice for colorful and high-textured vegetables; the powder adding a dash of spice to salad dressings and creamy egg dishes . . .

ABOVE: Far removed from the fields of mustard one sees in the countryside – mustard grown indoors can be eaten at the cotyledon stage, as a salad.

There are three types of mustard: *Brassica nigra*, black mustard, which can reach a height of 10 ft/3 m and was the main type grown commercially until some 40 years ago; *B. juncea*, brown mustard, which, growing to only 4½ ft/1.5 m, is more suitable for modern methods of harvesting; and *B. alba*, white mustard, a much milder form and the one beloved of school-children, who grow it as "mustard and cress."

The pungency of the herb is due to an essential oil which forms only when the dry mustard powder is mixed with water. It is not present in the dry seed – which is why the seed does not have the "bite" of made mustard – nor in the dry powder.

HISTORY

The Romans used mustard freely, soaking the dry seed in wine, and it is mentioned several times in the Bible. The name is thought to come from the Latin, *mustum ardens*, or burning must. Shakespeare includes several references to the herb, and places its commercial production accurately in Gloucestershire, a main centre of its growth, when he writes of "Tewkesbury mustard." It used to be ground by millers and sold as dry powder or paste in earthenware pots covered with parchment.

CHARACTERISTICS

Brown mustard, sometimes called juncea mustard, has a mass of small, four-petaled yellow flowers that form a dense carpet over the fields where they grow. It originates from China, India, and Poland. White mustard, which comes from the Mediterranean region, has a less distinctive flavor.

GROWING TIPS

All three types of mustard may be grown outdoors from seed sown in spring. It likes a moist soil and a sunny position. Harvest the seedpods in late summer, before they dry, and allow the seed to ripen in the pods. Store the seed in airtight jars, away from strong light. Seed may also be grown indoors. The traditional way for children to grow it is on a piece of folded cloth or blotting paper placed in a saucer or a glass jar and kept permanently moist. It will produce tasty and pungent shoots about 4 in/10 cm tall.

HOW TO USE

Mustard powder should be mixed with cold water. Boiling water kills the enzymes and produces a bitter flavor. Dry mustard powder is added to salad dressings to give them pungency, added to egg and cheese dishes, and can be rubbed over the skin of meat before roasting. White mustard seed is a preservative and is used in pickling, either alone or as an ingredient in mixed pickling spice.

Ready-made mustards vary according to regional traditions. Dijon mustard is made from black mustard seed mixed with wine and spices; Bordeaux mustard, which is dark brown, contains the seed husks; English ready-made mustard is usually a mixture of the black and white seeds, without the husk, blended with wheat flour. Whole-grain mustards, with their coarse granular texture, are becoming more popular.

A mustard bath, where the powder is mixed with hot water, is comforting for sore and aching feet and relaxing and reviving for the entire body.

Calendula officinalis
MARIGOLD

Marmalade-colored petals scattered over a green salad as a spicy garnish; whole flowers used in the medieval fashion to decorate dishes of meat and fish; the petals strewn into creamy custards to color them golden and add a hint of spice . . .

The sunshine-gold marigold flowers are a familiar sight in informal and country gardens and in colorful window boxes. The plant is a native of southern Europe but flourishes in cool, temperate climates. It was once treasured for its many culinary uses; the petals have a pungent, spicy flavor, and the leaves have a rather bitter aftertaste. A hardy annual, the marigold has a long flowering period, though not usually as long as its French popular name, *tous les mois*, would suggest.

HISTORY

Fresh or dried petals have been used as a saffron substitute since Roman times, and dried petals were sold from barrels by spice merchants in the Middle Ages for culinary and medicinal use.

CHARACTERISTICS

The plants can grow to a height of 9 in/23 cm, with a 6-in/15-cm spread. The pointed-oval leaves, which may be about 5 in/12 cm long, are slightly hairy. The flowers, either single or double, are brilliant yellow or bright orange with raised yellow centers.

LEFT: Common marigolds, *Calendula officinalis* – their daisy-shaped bright orange flowers are the stars of any mixed border.

ABOVE: Marigold petals give a piquant, spicy flavor to salads and, in the medieval way, may be scattered over desserts such as apple flan.

GROWING TIPS

A packet of marigold seed sown in the spring provides a sizeable bed or border edging of these vigorous plants. They like a rich, light soil and a sunny position, and grow well in planters and pots. Marigolds readily seed themselves.

HOW TO USE

The petals, with their slight aromatic bitterness, are used in fish and meat soups, rice dishes, cakes, desserts, and salads and, commercially, as a coloring for cheese and butter. In medieval times, the whole flowers were popular as a garnish.

Medicinally, the petals were used to heal wounds and to treat conjunctivitis, while the leaves were felt to relieve the effects of bee and wasp stings. An infusion of the petals may be used as a hair rinse to lighten fair hair, and the petals made into a nourishing cream for the skin. When used together with alum, the petals give a yellow dye.

CREAMY MARIGOLD CLEANSER

Ingredients
4 tbsp olive or almond oil
2 tbsp dried marigold flowers
few drops of violet, orange blossom or rose water

Preparation
● Warm the oil in a bowl placed over a saucepan of hot water. Stir in the dried flowers and continue to heat gently for 30 minutes.
● Remove the bowl from the heat and allow the oil to cool. Stir in the flower water.

MARIGOLD WINE

Ingredients
Yields 1 gal
2 qt marigolds (use *Calendula officinalis* only)
1 gal boiling water
1 Campden tablet, crushed
thinly pared rind and juice of 3 mandarins or other large, soft citrus
thinly pared rind and juice of 1 lemon
5¾ cups sugar
1½ cups golden raisins, finely chopped
wine yeast
yeast nutrient

Preparation
● Wash the flowers and put into a large container. Pour over the water, stir in the Campden tablet, and leave for 24 hours.
● Draw off 1 quart of the liquid, heat to just on boiling point with the citrus rind, then pour over the sugar, stirring until dissolved. Leave to cool to body temperature, then pour back into the bulk of the liquid together with the raisins, citrus juice, yeast and nutrient. Cover and leave in a warm place for 5 days to ferment, stirring twice a day.
● Strain the liquid through a double thickness of muslin. Pour into a fermenting jar, fitted with a fermentation lock, and leave to continue fermenting. Rack the wine as it begins to clear.
● When the wine is completely clear, bottle and store in a cool, dark, dry place for at least 6 months to mature.

Carum carvi
CARAWAY

Administered to both lovers and poultry in medieval times to prevent their straying; the seeds adding their pungent flavor to vegetables . . .

Caraway is a two-in-one plant. The bright green, feathery leaves have a mild flavor, somewhere between that of parsley and dill, while the seeds, a spice, have a strong aroma and pungent taste. The plant is grown commercially for its seed in northern Europe, the United States, and North Africa. A flavoring for use in baked goods and sweets is made from the essential oil distilled from the dry, ripe seed.

HISTORY

The plant was extensively used by the Romans and was well established in English kitchens in the Middle Ages, when it was cooked with fruit, especially spit-roast apples, and in cakes and bread. The leaves were chopped into soups and salads. In Germany and Austria – still the prime users of the plant – the seeds were cooked with vegetables, especially cabbage and its preserved form, sauerkraut.

CHARACTERISTICS

A biennial, the plant grows to a height of up to 24 in/60 cm, with a spread of 12 in/30 cm, and has thick, tapering roots rather like those of parsnip. The leaves resemble those of the carrot in shape. The flowers, in umbellifer clusters, are white tinged with pink and appear in midsummer. The pointed-oval seeds are dark brown, almost black.

GROWING TIPS

The seeds are sown outdoors in early autumn. They like a good soil and partial shade. They should be harvested, in the second year, just before they ripen. Hang them upside down to dry, the heads tied into a paper bag to catch the falling seeds.

ABOVE: A slender and straggly plant, caraway has delicate clusters of white flowers and small, feathery leaves.

LEFT: Caraway, one of a large family of umbellifers, is at its most effective when grown in a large clump.

HOW TO USE

The leaves may be used in salads and soups, the seeds in baked goods, in dumplings, cream cheese, and meat dishes such as goulash and pork casserole. The roots can be boiled as a vegetable and served with a white sauce. The leaves, seeds, and roots can be used as an aid to digestion.

TOP: Feverfew, whose pungent, bitter leaves are used in the treatment of migraine, has small, daisylike flowers.

ABOVE: With its bright, sharp green leaves, feverfew is an attractive border plant. Another form has even brighter leaves which are almost yellow.

Chrysanthemum parthenium
FEVERFEW

A few of the youngest, tenderest leaves made into sandwiches to ward off migraine; a tisane of fresh or dried leaves taken as a tonic; an infusion of the flowers patted lightly on the skin as a softener . . .

With its bright lime green or yellowy-green leaves that retain their color through the winter, feverfew is a year-round decorative garden plant. It is low growing, bushy, and vigorous, quickly thickening up, spreading, and self-seeding. The white flowers, which may be like single or double daisies, are particularly pretty and dry well for flower arranging.

HISTORY

Its medicinal uses are well chronicled by Gerard who, in his *Herball*, said that the dried plant was useful for those "that are giddie in the head . . . melancholike and pensive"; and by Culpeper, who recommended it for "all pains of the head coming of a cold cause."

CHARACTERISTICS

Various forms of the plant may grow to a height of anywhere from 9 in/22 cm to 24 in/60 cm. The deeply cut leaves are brightly colored, and have a sharp, unpleasantly bitter taste. The flowers, which are produced through the summer and into midautumn, are thick and daisylike, with yellow centers.

GROWING TIPS

The plant will thrive in the poorest of soils, even in paving cracks and walls. Ideally, it likes a well-drained soil and a sunny position. You can easily grow it from seed or by root division.

HOW TO USE

The plant's bitter taste rules out culinary uses, but is worth tolerating for its medicinal properties. The fresh or dried leaves can be particularly effective (made into sandwiches) as a cure for migraine, and as a tonic. The flowers are used in some skin preparations.

Coriandrum sativum
CORIANDER

The tiny round seeds crushed to a paste with chopped parsley and olive oil and rubbed into lamb before roasting; the seeds used to give the characteristic "bite" to mushrooms à la Grecque the leaves added just before serving spicy curries . . .

Both the green feathery leaves and the spherical seeds of coriander are indispensable in the kitchen, especially to anyone who is fond of curries. Bunches of coriander, which looks like flat-leaved parsley, are sold in many markets, especially where there is an Asian or Greek community. The seed is sold both whole or ground, and is a major ingredient in curry powder. It has a sweet taste reminiscent of orange peel.

HISTORY

Coriander seed was mentioned in the Bible, where it was likened to manna, but its use goes back much farther in time. The herb was used both in cooking and medicine in the ancient European cultures, and in South America, India, and China many thousands of years ago. The Romans took it to Britain, where it was much used in Elizabethan times.

CHARACTERISTICS

The plant grows to a height of 24 in/60 cm, with a spread of 9 in/22 cm. The bright green leaves are fan shaped and become more feathery toward the top of the plant. The flowers, which bloom from mid- to late summer, are small and white, formed in umbel-like clusters. The pale brown roots are fibrous and tapering, shaped rather like a carrot.

GROWING TIPS

A hardy annual, the plant is easy to grow from seed planted outdoors in late spring. It likes a light, well-drained soil and plenty of sun. Harvest the seed as soon as it starts to ripen, and hang the stems in paper bags to dry the seed.

HOW TO USE

The leaves do not dry well, but may be frozen. They are used in curries; ground to a paste with olive oil and the ground seed as a covering for roast lamb in marinades; sparingly – as they are rather bitter – in salads; and mixed with coconut and green chilies in a classic Indian chutney. The seeds, which may be roasted to bring out the full flavor, are widely used in curries and casseroles, in sausages, with fish and all *à la Grecque* dishes. They are also included in mixed pickling spice.

Medicinally, the herb may be taken as a digestive and for the treatment of colic.

ABOVE: Coriander leaves are used in the preparation of curries and many dishes of Middle-Eastern origin.

MARINATED KIPPER FILLETS

Ingredients

Serves 6 as an appetizer; 3 as a main dish

12 oz kipper fillets, or other smoked
fish fillets
1 medium onion, thinly sliced
2 tsp coriander seeds, crushed
2 bay leaves
freshly ground black pepper
¾ cup sunflower oil
4 tbsp red wine vinegar
1 tbsp brown sugar
grated rind of 1 lemon
2 tsp mustard powder
1 lemon, sliced
sprigs of fresh coriander

*The long marinating period revolutionizes the
flavor of the fish. Have a good supply of crusty
bread to mop up the delicious juices.*

Preparation

• Using a sharp knife, remove the skins from the kippers. Slice the kipper fillets diagonally into long strips. Layer in a shallow, wide dish, together with the onion, crushed coriander seeds, bay leaves, and black pepper.

• In a screw-top jar, shake together the oil, vinegar, brown sugar, lemon rind, and mustard powder until well blended and dissolved.

• Pour the dressing over the kipper fillets. Cover tightly with wrap and refrigerate for 2–5 days (the longer the better). Turn the fillets occasionally in the marinade.

• Serve garnished with lemon slices and sprigs of fresh coriander.

Dianthus caryophyllus
PINK

The flowers strewn in syrup to serve with fruit salads and compotes, or set in ice cubes to serve with tingling-cold summer drinks; the dried flowers – pink, red, crimson or white – added to a pot pourri for color and fragrance . . .

The garden pink or border carnation, romantically known as the gillyflower or July flower in Elizabethan and Victorian times, is a familiar and pretty cottage-garden plant. It grows wild in southern Europe and India, and has become naturalized in Britain. The flowers may be single or double, and come in all shades of pink and red, from shell pink to carmine.

HISTORY

The flowers have been used for cooking and perfumes for more than 2,000 years. In the Middle Ages, pinks were used in England as a clove substitute to spice wine and ale, when they were known as "sops."

CHARACTERISTICS

The plant grows to 12–24 in/30–60 cm, and may have a spread of 10 in/25 cm. The stems are erect, straight, and tough; the leaves long, slender, and grayish to silvery green. The flowers, about 1 in/2.5 cm across, are formed singly or in clusters and have a strong, clovelike aroma. Some have cut or intricately frilled petals and splashes or flashes of dual color. Many hybridized versions are available.

GROWING TIPS

The plant, a perennial, thrives in a poor but well-drained soil, and will even grow on walls or between paving stones. It may be grown from seed planted in late spring, but is more usually propagated by root division or layering in late summer.

HOW TO USE

The flowers have a sweet, spicy taste and are used to flavor syrups, especially for fruit salad, sauces, creams, jellies, butter, wine, fruit drinks, and salad dressings. They are candied to decorate cakes and desserts, and used to garnish salads.

They may be used to scent toilet waters, and in pot pourri and herbal sleep pillows.

ABOVE : A patch of
delicately colored
dianthus or pinks is a
perfect edging for an
herbaceous border or
herb garden.

Foeniculum vulgare
FENNEL

The soft threadlike leaves wrapped around herring or mackerel for baking, chopped into a stuffing to cook with trout, or used generously in a marinade for pork; the seeds baked with chopped black olives in savory bread to serve on a platter, with cheese and cold beer . . .

With its umbels of minute yellow flowers and dark green or bronze wispy leaves, fennel is a decorative addition to a herbaceous border, where, because of its size, it makes a good background plant. For centuries the herb has been associated in cooking with fish and used medicinally as a digestive. The seeds are chewed as a breath freshener, particularly appropriate after eating curries. Sweet or Roman fennel, the herb, should not be confused with Florence fennel (*finocchio*), the vegetable grown for its creamy-white bulbous root.

HISTORY

Fennel is native to southern Europe, and was extensively used by the Romans. Its use in England was widespread before the Norman conquest. Its partnership with fish was so well established, on fast days poor people are said to have eaten the fennel without the fish.

CHARACTERISTICS

The plant dominates any border, growing to a height of 5 ft/1.5 m, with a spread of 2½ ft/75 cm. The stems are pale green, multibranched, and ridged. The leaves,

soft and frondy, are formed like giant hands and have an aniselike flavor. The seeds – which are flat, ridged, and oval – form in late summer and have a more pronounced taste.

GROWING TIPS

Seed may be sown "on site" in spring, and the developing plants should be thinned to 2 ft/60 cm apart; or existing plants – hardy perennials – may be increased by root division. They like a well-drained soil and a sunny position.

HOW TO USE

The leaves are used with pork, veal and fish, in fish stock, sauces and stuffings, and in mayonnaise and salad dressings. The dried stalks are placed under broiled or barbecued fish to impart flavor. The seeds are used as a spice, particularly in bread, savory biscuits, and crackers. At the two-leaf (cotyledon) stage, the seedlings make a pungent salad, reminiscent of mustard.

Medicinally, the leaves and dried seeds are used for flatulence and in gripe waters, which are still popular for babies' colic, while an infusion of the leaves may be used for eyestrain.

L E F T : Its tall, curving stems and its dense cluster of soft feathery leaves make fennel and bronze fennel ideal back-of-the-border plants.

BAKED FISH WITH LIME & HERB BUTTER

Ingredients
Serves 4
2 oz butter
4 medium or 1 large fish, cleaned
1 tsp fennel seeds
2 limes
1 ¼ cups medium-sweet red wine
salt and freshly ground black pepper
sprigs of fresh fennel
Oven temperature: 400°F.

The subtle flavors of fennel and lime blend beautifully with red mullet, snapper, or rainbow trout. For a delicious variation, substitute orange and vermouth for the lime and wine.

Preparation
● Preheat the oven. Lightly butter a shallow oven-proof dish. Place the fish in the bottom. Dot with the remaining butter and then sprinkle with the fennel seeds.
● Using a vegetable peeler, cut several strips of the lime rind and put among the fish. Squeeze over the juice of the limes and pour the wine over the fish.
● Season well with salt and freshly ground black pepper. Cover tightly with foil and bake for about 25 minutes, or until the fish is cooked through and flakes easily when tested with the tip of a knife.
● Serve the fish with some of its juices, garnished with a few sprigs of fresh fennel and topped with a slice of chilled butter mixed with herbs, if desired.

A B O V E : Pluck off a few of the long, slender hyssop leaves for use in salads, sausages and casseroles.

A B O V E   R I G H T : A dense, healthy hyssop plant, its leaves a tender green, is a fine sight in any herb garden.

Hyssopus officinalis
HYSSOP

Fresh leaves used sparingly as a scatter-garnish for tomato or cucumber salads; the bright blue flowers used, as they were generations ago, to garnish cold meat dishes . . .

This decorative and long-lasting herb is an attractive one to grow. Native to southern Europe, the Near East, and southern Russia, it is a garden escape in the United States. It has a slightly bitter flavor with over tones of mint, and was so widely known in ancient times Dioscorides wrote that it needed no description.

HISTORY

Hyssop was used in all the Mediterranean countries in pre-Christian times, and is mentioned in the Bible. In his *Herball*, Gerard records that he grew all kinds in his garden; while Culpeper recommended it, boiled with figs, as an excellent gargle. In self-help medicine, a tisane of fresh or dried hyssop leaves was taken as a cure for rheumatism.

CHARACTERISTICS

The plant grows to 24 in/60 cm tall, with a spread of around half that. The leaves are about 1 in/2.5 cm long, pointed oval, and dark green. The flowers, which bloom from midsummer to midautumn, are mauvish blue, ¼ in/6 mm long, and carried in long, narrow spikes. The stems, flowers, and leaves all give off a strong aroma.

GROWING TIPS

The plant, a sub-shrub, enjoys a dry, well-drained soil, and a sunny position. It can be grown from seed planted in spring, from root divisions, or from tip cuttings taken before flowering. The shrub needs protection in severe winters, and may need replacing every five years or so.

HOW TO USE

The fresh or dried leaves and flowers may be added to soups, ragouts, casseroles, and sausages. Fresh leaves may be used sparingly in salads. The herb is an ingredient of Chartreuse liqueur.

Medicinally, hyssop is used for coughs, colds, bronchitis, and as a gargle for sore throats. Fresh and dried leaves were used as a strewing herb, and may be used in pot pourri, in insect-repellent sachets, and in rinsing water for laundry.

Iris germanica
ORRIS ROOT

The dried powder, with its fragrance of sweet violets, used as a fixative in the making of pot pourri, sleep pillow blends and lavender-bag mixtures . . .

Spectacular as the flowers are, it is the root or rhizome of the Florentine iris that is the valuable part of the plant. The name (orris) derives from the Greek word for rainbow, indicating the range of flower colors.

HISTORY

Orris root originates from southern Europe, and became naturalized in Iran and northern India. It has been identified in a wall painting of an Egyptian temple dating from 1500 BC. It was at one time used as a purgative, but is not now used medicinally.

CHARACTERISTICS

The long and slender plant grows to a height of 3 ft/90 cm, while its straight, fleshy, and erect stems are wrapped in long, pointed, sword-shaped leaves. The flowers are about 4 in/10 cm across, and may be white, tinged with mauve or with a yellow beard. The bulbous and fleshy rhizome is white under the skin and smells strongly of violets. The plant has small fibrous roots.

GROWING TIPS

The rhizomes are divided in late spring and should be taken with a bud or shoot in place. They prefer deep, fertile, well-drained soil and a position in full sun. They should be planted half above and half below the soil, and divided every four or five years. For dried orris root, lift the rhizomes in autumn and hang them in a warm place. The fragrance develops as the rhizomes wither and dry.

HOW TO USE

The ground powder made from the dried root is used as a fixative in pot pourri, in talcum powder, bath preparations, and dry shampoos.

LEFT: The dried root of the iris plant, known as orris root, is used as a fixative in pot pourri blends.

ABOVE LEFT: The long, sword-shaped leaves of *Iris germanica* form a neat, tight fan shape as they grow.

A B O V E : The pointed-oval, glossy leaves of the bay tree are a fragrant addition to sweet and savory dishes of all kinds.

Laurus nobilis
BAY

A spray of bay leaves garnishing the top of a glazed terrine; a fresh or dried leaf flavoring a hearty stew or a delicate custard; the dried leaves bound on to a twig ring to make an evergreen kitchen decoration . . .

Bay leaves are among the most versatile of herbs, and the plants, if regularly clipped, rank among the most decorative of shrubs. The glossy and sweetly scented leaves are indispensable in both French and Mediterranean cooking, a traditional ingredient in bouquet garni, and a "must" in marinades, *court bouillon*, stocks, and pickles.

HISTORY

The bay tree came originally from Asia Minor, and was established around the ancient cultures of the Mediterranean. Dedicated to the god Apollo, it was the laurel referred to in the crown of laurel leaves presented as a symbol of wisdom and victory in ancient Greece and Rome, the origin of the circlet of leaves worn by victorious motor racing drivers today. The French word *baccalaureat*, for examinations, and the term "bachelor," for academic degrees, both derive from the Latin for laurel berry, *bacca laureus*.

CHARACTERISTICS

Bay leaves are flat, pointed oval, about 3 in/7.5 cm long, dark green, and glossy. They retain a somewhat balsamic scent, and the wood, too, is strongly aromatic. In ideal conditions, the shrubby trees may grow to 25 ft/7.5 m tall and up to 6 ft/2 m across. The stems are tough and woody, and have a gray bark. The flowers, which appear in late spring, are small, yellow, and rather insignificant.

GROWING TIPS

Propagation is by heel cuttings, taken in early summer and kept under cover. Young trees are best planted out in spring; they like good, well-drained soil and a sunny, sheltered position. Harsh winter weather can kill them if they are left too exposed. For this reason, bay is often grown against a wall, or in pots or tubs. The trees can be clipped into neat topiary shapes, the sphere being the most traditional, and are often used decoratively on a porch, terrace, or in a garden room.

HOW TO USE

Bay leaves are used in all branches of cooking – in soups, stews, casseroles, stocks, syrups, sweet and savory sauces, and as a garnish. An infusion of the leaves may be taken for flatulence, and the dried leaves are crumbled into pot pourri. To dry the leaves, simply hang them in bunches in a warm, dry place.

L E F T : Left to its own devices, a bay tree will spread far and wide. The trees are perfect candidates for clipping into neat topiary shapes.

PATATAS BRAVAS

Ingredients
Serves 4
1 onion, chopped
2 tbsp olive oil
1 bay leaf
2 red chilies
2 tsp crushed garlic
1 tbsp tomato paste
1 tbsp sugar
1 tbsp soy sauce
1 lb can plum tomatoes, chopped
1 glass of white wine
salt and black pepper
8 medium potatoes
Oven temperature: 450°F.

The sauce for this dish should be slightly sweet and the flavor of the tomatoes should not dominate it.

Preparation
● To make the sauce, sweat the onions in the oil with the bay leaf.
● When soft, add the chilies, garlic, tomato paste, sugar, and soy sauce. Sweat for another 5 minutes on low heat.
● Add the chopped tomatoes and white wine. Stir, bring to a boil and simmer for 10 minutes. Season to taste.
● To prepare the potatoes, cut as you would for roast potatoes. Place the potatoes on a greased baking tray, season well and brush with melted butter. Roast in the hot oven until golden.
● Reheat the tomato sauce, pour over the potatoes and serve immediately.

OPPOSITE: Whether grown commercially in a field, as a dense hedge or as a border plant, lavender is one of the most attractive and fragrant of herbs.

RIGHT: Lavender flowers have many culinary, cosmetic and domestic uses, and are an invaluable ingredient in pot pourri.

Lavandula angustifolia
LAVENDER

Bunches of lavender hanging to dry in a corner; a basket of headily scented lavender flowers decorating a bedroom or bathroom; a "bouquet" of flowers strewn in syrup to pour over sweet cakes and pastries . . .

Lavender is a traditional cottage-garden plant, its gray-green spiky foliage and spires of mauvy-blue flowers providing color throughout the year. It is native to the Mediterranean and grows in profusion in the sun-baked *maquis* region of southern France.

HISTORY

The Greeks and Romans used this highly aromatic plant to make perfumes and ointments. Since the Middle Ages, the dried flowers have been one of the main ingredients of pot pourri; fresh sprigs were included in herbal bunches, known as tussie mussies, to mask unpleasant household odors and ward off fevers. Bunches of lavender were sold on city streets in Victorian times. "Won't you buy my pretty lavender?" was one of the traditional street cries of London.

CHARACTERISTICS

The plant may grow to a height of 3 ft/90 cm, but there are dwarf forms for edging which reach only about 10 in/25 cm. The stems are thick and woody, and become straggly if left unpruned. The leaves are long (about 3 in/7.5 cm), spiky, and very narrow. The tiny tubular flowers are carried on long spikes in thick round-the-stem clusters. The fibrous roots are shallow and wide spreading.

GROWING TIPS

Propagation of this evergreen shrub is by cuttings taken in spring or late summer. The plants like a dry, well-drained, and preferably stony soil and a warm, sunny position. They should be lightly pruned in spring. Harvest the spikes just as the flowers begin to open, and hang them upside down to dry.

HOW TO USE

Fresh lavender flowers may be used to flavor syrup for gelatin and fruit salads, and milk and cream for desserts. They may also be candied to decorate cakes and puddings. Fresh or dried flowers are used in rinsing water for clothes and hair. Bunches of lavender are said to ward off insects, and an infusion of the flowers may help relieve insect bites. Because of their sweet, pungent smell, the dried flowers and seeds are a frequent ingredient of pot pourris, herbal sleep pillows, and sachets. Dried lavender stems are used to weave decorative baskets and bowls.

SIMPLE LAVENDER SOAP

Ingredients
10 tbsp finely grated castille soap
8 tbsp boiling water
2 tbsp crushed dried lavender flowers
4 drops of lavender oil

Preparation
• Melt the soap in the water in a bowl placed over a saucepan of hot water, stirring frequently, until smooth.
• Crush the flowers to a powder and take the bowl off the saucepan of hot water. Stir the flowers into the soap with the oil.
• Pour into a bottle and label.

RIGHT: Lovage, which grows to a height of 5 ft/1.5 m, is a tall, stately plant topped by clusters of greenish yellow flowers.

BELOW: The large, fleshy leaves of lovage may be lightly cooked as a vegetable, and the stems candied and used in the same way as angelica.

Levisticum officinale
LOVAGE

A clear, sparkling meat broth flavored with young lemon-scented shoots of lovage; a sauce made with the chopped leaves and served with poached white fish; the celery-flavored seeds baked in crackers to serve with cheese . . .

Lovage was much used as a herb in Britain during the Middle Ages, and then, like so many others, went out of fashion for several centuries. It is the tallest of the umbellifers, reaching over 6 ft/1.8 m, and makes an attractive back-of-the-border addition. All parts of the plant – leaves, stems, and seeds – can be used in the kitchen, and so it well repays its keep.

HISTORY

A native of southern Europe, lovage was known to the Greeks and Romans, and was recommended by Culpeper in his mid-17th-century herbal. He advised that the bruised leaves, fried in hog's lard and applied hot to the area, will quickly break "any blotch or boil." The herb was once thought to be an aphrodisiac, and was used by witches in their love potions.

CHARACTERISTICS

With its bright green, hand-shaped leaflets and thickly ridged hollow stems, the plant looks rather like over-grown celery, and gives off a distinct celerylike aroma. The flowers, which bloom in mid- to late summer, are small, yellow, and formed in umbrellalike clusters. The seeds are flat, oval and deeply ridged. The plant reaches a height of 5 ft/1.5 m.

GROWING TIPS

Seed of this herbaceous perennial is sown outdoors in spring for transplanting in the autumn. It may also be propagated by root cuttings. It enjoys a good, moist soil and a position in partial shade.

HOW TO USE

The leaves may be used to flavor soups, casseroles, sauces, and marinades, or lightly cooked as a green vegetable. The stems are candied as angelica, and the seeds are often used to flavor bread, savory biscuits, and crackers.

An infusion can be used as a diuretic, to relieve flatulence, and as an antiseptic.

Melissa officinalis
LEMON BALM

The bright yellow-green leaves strewn in syrup for fruit salads and compotes; floating in white wine or strawberry cups; scattered over green salad, or shaken, just before serving, in salad dressings to impart a lemony flavor . . .

Balm is an attractive herb with yellow or variegated leaves smelling strongly of lemons. It is a great addition to any garden since it maintains a strong attraction for bees. Indeed, it used to be said that a swarm of bees would never desert a hive if a lemon balm plant were close by. A tisane made from the leaves, known as melissa tea, is said to relieve tiredness, sooth headaches, and have a calming effect on the nerves. In this capacity, it was a popular drink with Victorian ladies.

HISTORY

Lemon balm is native to southern Europe and has been cultivated for over 2,000 years. The Romans brought it to Britain, where it was widely grown in the Middle Ages, during which time melissa honey was popular as a sugar substitute.

CHARACTERISTICS

The plant is a vigorous grower that will readily spread through the border. It reaches a height of 3 ft/90 cm, with a spread of 24 in/60 cm. The oval, almost heart-shaped, leaves have slightly serrated edges and a pronounced network of veins; they can be up to 2½ in/ 6 cm long and 1½ in/4 cm across. The flowers, which bloom from mid- to late summer are small, white, and insignificant.

GROWING TIPS

It is a good idea to grow lemon balm in sunken pots or other containers to prevent unwanted spreading. The plant is a perennial that dies down in winter. It is grown from seed sown outdoors in spring, or from root division. It prefers a moist, fertile soil and partial shade.

HOW TO USE

The fresh leaves may be used in salads, candied for cake decoration, and used to garnish fish and other dishes. Add them at the last minute to summer drinks and fruit salads – after long infusion they turn unpleasantly brown – and, in recipes, as a lemon peel substitute. An infusion of the leaves makes a refreshing skin toner and can be used in water to rinse clothes. The dry leaves lend a refreshing lemony scent to pot pourri blends.

ABOVE: Just brush against the soft, downy leaves of lemon balm and you release the powerful aroma of citrus fruits.

ABOVE LEFT: Lemon balm is a vigorous plant which will colonize a border or herb patch if the roots are not contained.

Mentha pulegium
PENNYROYAL

Hearty chunks of black pudding flavored with pennyroyal and served with crusty local bread; herby sausages aromatic with its strong and mintlike flavor; a few dried leaves added to "linen bags" to hang in closets . . .

Pennyroyal, a herbaceous perennial and a close relation of mint, has a strong, bitter, minty taste some people find unpleasant. It has a completely different growing habit than mint, its prostrate stems creeping along the ground and forming an effective, dense ground cover that can be used as a lawn. It is a native of Europe where it grows freely in damp, shady places and is also found in North and South America.

HISTORY

In spite of its bitter aroma and flavor, pennyroyal was widely used as a culinary herb by the Greeks and Romans. It had its domestic uses, too, and, as its name implies (*pulegium* is derived from *pulex*, the Latin for flea), was used as an insect repellent.

CHARACTERISTICS

Each prostrate plant is capable of spreading at least 12 in/30 cm along the ground. The leaves, around ¼–½ in/6–12 mm long, are dark green, oval, and may be toothed. The flowers, which appear from mid- to late summer, are purple and borne in tight clusters at leaf joints around the stem.

GROWING TIPS

Pennyroyal needs plenty of moisture, but will tolerate a poor soil. It will even grow in the cracks of paving stones if kept well watered. It can be grown from seed planted in late spring under cover, or from rooted shoots planted in spring or autumn. It will tolerate full sun or partial shade.

HOW TO USE

The leaves may be used sparingly in place of mint, but have more application medicinally and domestically. They can be used to relieve insect bites and stings, to ward off insects – as a moth repellent in drawers, for instance – and in the treatment of headaches, colds, and sickness. The leaves have been used as a strewing herb, and in laundry rinsing water.

Note that pennyroyal should not be taken during the months of pregnancy.

RIGHT: In days gone by, the tiny, rounded leaves of pennyroyal were used as a strewing herb and as an aromatic rinse for laundry.

Mentha spicata
GARDEN MINT

A leaf or two of new season's mint added to new potatoes and peas in celebration of the first young crops; marrow baked Greek-style with a rice and mint stuffing; candied young sprigs to decorate cakes and desserts . . .

There are many species and types of this most popular of culinary herbs.

Spearmint, or garden mint, is the most commonly grown "domestic" mint, which, according to variety, may have dark green or gray-green leaves with smooth, decorative, or frilled edges; eau-de-cologne mint (*M. citrata*) has the scent of orange flowers and numbers orange, lavender, and bergamot mints among its varieties; water mint (*M. aquatica*) and horse mint (*M. longifolia*) grow in the wild and have an over-poweringly strong aroma; while round-leaved mint

(*M. rotundifolia*) has a distinctive appearance and numbers apple mint, Bowles, and pineapple mints in its list of varieties.

Most species are native to the Mediterranean region and western Asia, and now grow wild throughout northern Europe and in parts of North America. They will grow wild in the garden, too, if their roots are not contained (in a bottomless container sunk into the ground, say) and their colonization process curtailed by vigilant thinning and cutting back.

HISTORY

Mint was used extensively by the Greeks and Romans. Pliny said of it that "the smell . . . does stir up the mind and the taste to a greedy desire of meat." And it was the Romans who introduced both spearmint and mint sauce to Britain.

CHARACTERISTICS

The plants, herbaceous perennials, may grow to a

ABOVE: A selection of mints: 1 apple mint; 2 variegated apple mint; 3 black peppermint; 4 white peppermint; 5 ginger mint; 6 lemon mint; 7 basil mint; 8 eau-de-cologne mint; 9 curly garden mint.

height of over 18 in/45 cm, with a spread of 12 in/ 30 cm. They have tough, vigorous roots and stems, which creep beneath the ground and establish new plants along the way. The small, bluish-mauve flowers, which tend to bloom late in the summer, are borne in clusters on cylindrical spires.

GROWING TIPS

Propagation comes from planting the runners, which produce numerous shoots, in spring. The plants are perennial but the foliage dies in autumn, the time to trim the plants and surround them with a mulch of rotted leaves or lawn cuttings. If the plants are attacked by rust they should be burned and fresh ones started in another part of the garden.

HOW TO USE

Mint sauce, in which the chopped herb is mixed with vinegar as a accompaniment to roast lamb, is the traditional herald of a British spring. A sprig of mint can be added when cooking new potatoes, peas, marrow, and many other vegetables. Mint is chopped into softened butter for serving with lamb; and into apple jelly as a preserve to serve with a variety of poultry, meats and broiled fish. Sprigs of mint are also used as a garnish, and to flavor fruit salads and summer drinks, particularly mint julep. Mint tea, served hot or cold with a slice of lemon, is a refreshing and reviving tisane. The dried leaves may be used in pot pourri.

GRAPEFRUIT MINT SORBET

Ingredients
Serves 6
1 small lemon
1½ cups water
⅞ cup sugar
a handful of fresh mint leaves,
stripped from their stalks
2 good-sized grapefruit
2 egg whites
pinch salt

Preparation
• Pare the lemon in strips with a potato peeler and put the rind in a small pan with 1 cup of the water and half the sugar. Stir, bring to a boil and simmer for 6 minutes.
• Take off the heat, add the mint (garden or apple mint) and leave to cool.
• Finely grate ½ of the rind from one of the grapefruits and reserve. Squeeze the grapefruits and lemon, and mix with the syrup.
• Strain into a shallow metal dish and freeze until just firm, beating a couple of times.
• Cook the remaining sugar and water over a low heat. When the bottom of the pan no longer feels "gritty" when tapped with a wooden spoon, turn up the heat and boil for 5 minutes.
• Meanwhile, whisk the egg whites with the salt until they form stiff peaks. Pour on the boiling sugar syrup in a thin stream, beating all the while.
• Cool over cold water or ice cubes, beating from time to time, then beat in the grapefruit ice, broken up, and the finely grated rind. Freeze.
• Serve garnished with fresh mint sprigs.

Monarda didyma
BERGAMOT

Bergamot tea, a tisane with a history, taken as a soothing and relaxing drink; the leaves used to garnish fruit drinks and wine cups; and dried to add a hint of spice to various pot pourri blends . . .

The bergamots are very much an American herb, native to North America and widely used by the American Indians. The plant has a pleasant smell of oranges and, with its red, pinky-red, or purple flowers, is an attractive addition to any border. It is strongly attractive to bees. Besides the most common red bergamot, there is wild bergamot (*M. fistulosa*), native to southern Canada and the northern United States, and lemon bergamot (*M. citriodora*), which, too, has a strong citrus aroma.

HISTORY

Bergamot was used by the Oswega Indians, and Oswega tea was made by colonists at the time of the Boston Tea Party in order to boycott British imports.

CHARACTERISTICS

The plant, a herbaceous perennial, will grow to a height of 3 ft/90 cm, with a spread of over 12 in/ 30 cm. The fibrous roots form a thick, dense block.

The dark green leaves, which may be tinged with red, are hairy and up to 6 in/15 cm long. The flowers, up to 2 in/5 cm long, are borne in thick clusters at the top of the stem from mid- to late summer.

GROWING TIPS

The plants may be grown from seed planted in spring or from root divisions taken in spring or autumn. They like a sunny position and moist but well-drained soil.

HOW TO USE

Fresh leaves may be used sparingly in salads, fruit salad, and fruit drinks, and fresh or dried leaves made into a refreshing and relaxing tea that is said to be soporific. The dried leaves lend a pleasantly citrus aroma to pot pourri blends.

A B O V E : With its spectacular scarlet flowers and its citruslike aroma, bergamot contributes much to the herb garden.

Myrrhis odorata
SWEET CICELY

A succulent salad of sweet cicely roots lightly boiled and served with a vinaigrette or creamy dressing; a fruit salad given the slightly anise flavor of the leaves; a summer flower arrangement enhanced by the long stems of fluffy cream-colored flowers . . .

Sweet cicely grows wild in northern Europe, and contributes much visually to a border or herb garden. With its large, bright-green, lacy leaves and mass of creamy-white flowers borne on huge umbel-like clusters, it makes a perfect back-of-the-border plant, reaching in some cases a height of 5 ft/1.5 m. It is in full leaf from very early spring until midwinter, after most herbs have died back, and is therefore especially useful. The whole plant of this herbaceous perennial is fragrant, with a mildly aniseed aroma that complements fruit dishes and fruit salads. The leaves do not dry well and are best used fresh.

RIGHT: Sweet cicely, which grows to a height of 6 ft/1.8 m, blends well with tall border plants such as foxgloves and hollyhocks.

BELOW: The bright green, fernlike leaves of sweet cicely are delicious when used in salads and fruit salads.

HISTORY

In his *Herball*, Gerard stated that when the seeds were eaten with oil, vinegar, and pepper they "exceed all other salads." The botanical name of the plant is thought to recognize that the leaves have an aroma similar to that of myrrh, and the popular name indicates its sweet flavor. To this end, in medieval times it was used in fruit dishes as a sugar substitute.

CHARACTERISTICS

The plant is so decorative, neat, and tidy, it easily earns a place in a flower border, where it may spread to 3 ft/90 cm across and grows to twice that height. The thick, hollow stems are deeply ridged, while the leaves, pale on the undersides, are toothed and fern-like, and up to 12 in/30 cm long. The flowers appear in late spring and early summer, are attractive to bees, and number among the prettiest of the umbellifers. The roots are long, thick, and fleshy, and, like a parsnip, white inside a light brown skin. The seeds, which may be up to 1 in/2.5 cm long, are brownish black, long, narrow, and sharply pointed.

GROWING TIPS

The seeds are slow to germinate, and so it is best to grow the plant from root division; a small piece of root with an eye is all you need. Plant it 2½ in/6 cm deep in spring where it is to grow. Transplanting is difficult, because the roots are deeply penetrative. It enjoys a deep, moist soil and partial shade.

HOW TO USE

The leaves may be used fresh in salads and fruit salads, and chopped into other fruit dishes such as pies and compotes. The peeled roots can be boiled and eaten as a vegetable, accompanied by a white sauce or vinaigrette dressing. The seeds are used in the making of the well-known Chartreuse liqueur.

Nepeta cataria
CATMINT

A plant of spreading catmint in the border as a comfort patch for the feline population; a few leaves used cautiously in salads; a tisane made from fresh or dried leaves and taken when relaxation is the order of the day . . .

Catmint, the herb so attractive to the feline population, has few culinary uses. With its gently curved spikes of heart-shaped gray-green leaves and clusters of white or pale blue flowers, it is, however, an attractive addition to a border.

HISTORY

The plant, a herbaceous perennial, is native to Asia and Europe, and was widely used in self-help medicines. In his herbal, Gerard recommends it for colds, coughs, chest complaints, and nervousness.

CHARACTERISTICS

The plant grows to a height of up to 3 ft/90 cm, with a spread of 15 in/38 cm. It has a straggly habit, and is liable to be squashed flat by cats rolling on it. Indeed, to preserve plants from this inevitable fate, it may be necessary to protect them with wire netting.

GROWING TIPS

Catmint can be grown from seed planted in spring or summer in good fertile soil in partial shade, or by root division or cuttings taken in spring.

HOW TO USE

The fresh leaves, which have a very strong aroma, can be used sparingly in salads. A tisane made from the leaves and flowers may be taken for coughs, colds, and catarrh, and is noted as a soothing bedtime drink.

RIGHT: Catmint is distinguished by the small mauve flowers which form just above the pairs of leaves at the top of the long, straight stems.

LEFT: It is advisable to protect clumps of catmint by wires or an enclosing circle of wire netting to prevent cats from rolling on them.

Ocimum basilicum
SWEET BASIL

A glistening tomato salad made all the more piquant and colorful for a scattering of torn basil leaves; large leaves wrapped around whole fish for broiling or baking; roast chicken cooked with a basil and orange stuffing . . .

With a pot of basil on the windowsill and a tomato plant in a window box outside, you have the perfect partnership for many summer salads, sauces and casseroles, for basil and tomatoes go together in any combination you care to mention. The herb is a half-hardy annual emanating from warm climates and is therefore a sun-lover. With care and adequate heat, a plant will stay in leaf indoors right through to midwinter, a luxury for those who love to use their herbs fresh. You can freeze basil, or preserve it in the Italian way, the leaves packed into jars with rock salt and olive oil.

HISTORY

Basil traveled overland to Europe via the Middle East from India, where it is considered sacred by the Hindus. A Belgian old wives' tale of the 16th century told that basil leaves crushed between two bricks would turn into scorpions, while Boccaccio has his heroine Lisabetta burying her lover's head in a pot of basil and watering it with her tears.

CHARACTERISTICS

According to type, a basil plant can have either a multitude of minute leaves or ones up to 4 in/10 cm long and almost half as wide, glossy, smooth, silky, and highly aromatic – they smell something like cloves. The stems tend to be woody and straggly, and the flowers, in long spikes, are small, white, and tubular. They appear from midsummer through to the autumn. The plants can reach a height of 2 ft/60 cm.

GROWING TIPS

Basil is the ideal windowsill herb, but will grow satisfactorily outdoors if sheltered from the wind. Sow seed shallowly in gentle heat in late spring and transplant toward midsummer, taking care not to disturb the roots. It likes a moist but well-drained soil and plenty of sun. Pinch out the tips of the shoots to prevent flowering and encourage bushy growth. Harvest by taking the larger, lower leaves first.

HOW TO USE

In Italy and France, basil is used to make, respectively, *pesto* or *pistou* sauce (see recipe), in which it is crushed with garlic and pinenuts. The sauce may be served with spaghetti or stirred into soup. Basil is good not only with tomatoes, but with sweet peppers, eggplant, and zucchini; with chicken, eggs, and steak (when it is pounded with softened butter and drizzled over the meat). Medicinally, it may be used as a mild sedative and to relieve stomach pains and sickness. A pot of basil in the kitchen is said to discourage flies.

LEFT: This patio container has been planted with two distinct varieties of basil, together with some parsley and chives.

PESTO SAUCE

Ingredients
Serves 4
1 oz fresh basil leaves
2 cloves garlic, crushed
pinch of salt
⅓ cup pine nuts
½ cup parmesan cheese
½ cup olive oil

Preparation
● Blend the basil leaves in a liquidizer. If your supply of basil is insufficient, combine fresh parsley and basil for a slightly different flavor.
● Add the garlic and olive oil and process for a few seconds.
● Gradually add the pine nuts, parmesan cheese and season, remembering that parmesan has a salty taste. The consistency should be thick and creamy.
● This quantity of pesto is sufficient for 1 lb cooked drained pasta. Mix 2 tbsp pesto with the pasta and serve on individual plates with an extra spoonful of pesto on each helping.

Origanum majorana
SWEET MARJORAM

Anchovies dressed with lemon juice, olive oil, and sweet marjoram leaves to serve as an appetizer; eggs baked under a light covering of light cream and chopped marjoram; grilled meats generously sprinkled with the dried herb and cooked to a sizzling brown . . .

Sweet or knotted marjoram is highly perfumed and has thick trusses of dainty white, pale mauve, or purple flowers, which make it one of the most decorative plants in the herb garden. It can be used in many ways since the leaves dry or freeze well for culinary use, and the flowers may be dried for long-lasting arrangements or pot pourri. In warm climates, where it originates, sweet marjoram is a perennial, but it must be treated as a half-hardy annual in colder conditions, since it will not survive severe winters.

HISTORY

Sweet marjoram has been cultivated since ancient times. It is a native of central Europe, where it was grown for its many medicinal uses.

CHARACTERISTICS

The plant grows to about 10 in/25 cm high, with a spread of 8 in/20 cm. The stems are tough, woody, and inclined to be straggly, while the dark grayish-green leaves are oval and up to ¾ in/20 mm long. The flowers are minute but plentiful, and are borne in clusters around the stem. They are produced from green pealike buds known as "knots," which give the plant its alternative name.

GROWING TIPS

The plant prefers a moist, fertile soil in a sunny position that is sheltered from wind. Sow seed in late spring when there is no risk of frost. To aid germination, which in cold soil can take a month, it is a good idea to warm the soil first by protecting it with cloches.

HOW TO USE

Add fresh leaves to casseroles just before serving to retain the full flavor. They can also be used in sauces, stuffings, sparingly in salads, in egg and cheese dishes, and in fruit salads. Medicinally, the plant may be taken as a digestive, and it is useful in the home as an insect repellent. With their sweet, pungent aroma, the dried leaves and flowers are good in pot pourri and herbal sleep pillows. Hang the flower stems upside down in a warm, airy place to dry them for arranging.

HISTORY

The plant originates from the Mediterranean region, where its pungency is in direct proportion with its quota of sun. It is a traditional ingredient of Mexican chili powder, and has long been used as a flavoring for chili sauces and chili beans.

CHARACTERISTICS

This hardy annual grows to a height of about 8 in/ 20 cm, with woody stems and dark green leaves around ¾ in/20 mm long. The flowers, borne on long spikes, are small and white in color.

GROWING TIPS

The plant demands a well-drained soil in full sun, though a poor, stony soil will be adequate. Plant seed in warm soil in late spring, or, in midspring, in pots or seed trays under glass. Oregano does especially well in indoor mini-propagators placed on the windowsill.

HOW TO USE

The fresh leaves, which are sold in bundles in Italian and Greek markets, are useful additions to salads, casseroles (toward the end of cooking), soups, sauces, pâtés, and poultry dishes. Dried oregano is especially good with tomatoes, beans, eggplant, zucchini, and rice, and in dishes such as pilaf and risotto.

Origanum vulgare
OREGANO

Calamari soup rich with tomato and aromatic with fresh oregano leaves; chicken risotto with oregano stirred in at the point of serving; eggplant salad, melitzanesalata, *sprinkled with the fresh or dried herb for the unmistakable flavor of Greece . . .*

Oregano is a very close relative of marjoram, so much so there is some confusion in the cross-pollination of their names: what is known as marjoram in Britain turns up as oregano in Italy! This is the pungently aromatic herb of southern Italy, the one that is used, mainly in its dried form, to flavor pizzas and tomato sauces. Indeed, Greek cooks are convinced that dried oregano – *rigani* – is best used dried and, what's more, is the only herb worth drying!

ABOVE: Oregano, known as *rigani* in Greece, dries particularly well and retains its aroma for a long period of time.

ABOVE RIGHT: Later in the summer, this patch of oregano will be a mass of purple flowers which attract the bees and butterflies.

COTTABULLA

Ingredients
Serves 8
½ lb stale white bread, crusts removed
2 lb ground beef
2 medium onions, finely chopped
2 eggs
1 tsp ground coriander
1 tsp dried oregano
1 tbsp paprika
3 cloves of garlic, crushed
pinch of cayenne
1 tsp sugar
salt and freshly ground black pepper
Oven temperature: 375°F.

*Cottabulla, a dish of West Indian origin, is a tasty
cross between a cold meatloaf
and a pâté campagne.*

Preparation
● Soak the bread in water, squeeze out and crumble. Mix all the ingredients together thoroughly, seasoning with plenty of salt and pepper.
● Pack into a large soufflé dish leaving a slight hollow in the middle. Cover with foil and bake for 40 to 50 minutes until cooked through, but still slightly pink in the middle.
● While it is still hot, put a plate slightly smaller than the baking dish on top of the foil and weight it with some heavy cans. Leave until cold and firm, remove the weights and refrigerate until needed.
● To serve, slice into wedges. Cottabulla can also be served hot, in which case there is no need to weight it. Alternatively, shape the mixture into patties, roll in seasoned flour, and fry, broil or barbecue to make sensational hamburgers.

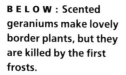

Pelargonium
SCENTED-LEAVED GERANIUM

A trio of lemon-scented leaves lining the base of a layer cake pan; a spray or two of the leaves decorating a red fruit gelatin salad; a few nutmeg-scented leaves strewn into the milk when making custard . . .

A pot of scented-leaved geranium in the kitchen is one of the most useful of herbs. You can put a couple of leaves in the base of a cake pan when making layer cakes or other baked goods, add a leaf or two to sauces, syrups, salads, and fruit salads, and use the pretty, sometimes variegated leaves for decorating and garnishing dishes of all kinds. The pelargonium species originate in South Africa, and are ideal for growing indoors. Outside, they are half-hardy perennials that collapse at the first touch of frost. Different varieties have different aromas. You can choose between lemon scented, *P. crispum minor*; apple scented, *P. odoratissimum*; oak-leaf scented, *P. quercifolium*; rose scented, *P. graveolens* and *P. radens*; nutmeg scented, *P. fragrans*; peppermint scented, *P. tomentosum*, and many others. The flowers – white, pink, mauve or red – are small and insignificant, and most have no smell.

HISTORY

The plants were "discovered" by Tradescant, the gardener of Charles I of England, and he grew a number of varieties in the royal greenhouses. One of the first to be brought to England was *P. triste*, which numbers among the few species that have scented flowers as well as foliage.

CHARACTERISTICS

The plants have dark green, pale green, or green-and-cream variegated leaves, which may be deeply cut or frilled and may vary in size from ½ in/12 mm to 3 in/7.5 cm across. The five-petaled flowers are borne in clusters and are long lived. Height varies considerably, and may be between 1 ft/30 cm and 3 ft/90 cm. The stems are tough and woody.

GROWING TIPS

Pelargonium are grown from tip cuttings taken under cover in spring and summer. They like a good well-drained soil, plenty of sun, and protection from cold. Grown indoors, they require plant food once a week to encourage full leaf growth. The plants should be cut back in winter to avoid their becoming straggly.

HOW TO USE

The fresh leaves may be infused in milk, cream, and syrups for desserts, sorbets, and ices; chopped into softened butter for sandwiches and cake fillings; and used extensively for garnishing. The dried leaves are a fragrant addition to pot pourri and sachets to scent clothes and linens; the fresh leaves can be infused in bath water or rinsing water for hair.

BELOW: Scented geraniums make lovely border plants, but they are killed by the first frosts.

BELOW: One of the many varieties of scented geranium, *Pelargonium crispum minor* smells of lemons.

ABOVE LEFT: Italian parsley, also known as flat-leaved parsley, has a sharper and more pronounced flavor than the curly-leaved type.

BELOW LEFT: The familiar curled-leaf parsley, which is widely used for garnishing meat, fish and vegetable dishes of all kinds, has a strong, almost sweet flavor.

Petroselinum crispum
PARSLEY

Rows of finely chopped parsley separating the light and dark meats in dressed crab; parsley sauce bringing out the subtle flavor of poached fish; parsley as one of the classic fines herbes *to flavor cheese and egg dishes . . .*

Parsley is an invaluable addition to bouquets garnis and *fines herbes* mixtures for grills and fish dishes. With its deep green, frilled or curly leaves, it is one of the best-known and most widely used herbs, as much for garnishing as for cooking. Italian parsley, whose flat leaves are reminiscent of coriander, is less decorative, has a sharper flavor, and is easier to grow.

HISTORY

A native of the eastern Mediterranean region, parsley was first recorded, in a Greek herbal, as long ago as the third century BC. It was used in ancient Rome in cooking and for ceremonial purposes. Pliny recorded that if scattered in a fish pond it had the power to cure unhealthy fish.

CHARACTERISTICS

The plant grows to a height of up to 18 in/45 cm, with a spread of 10 in/25 cm. The stems, which are also strongly aromatic, are green and supple, the leaves curled or flat. The flowers, which appear in the late summer of the plant's second year, are small and a yellowish green color.

GROWING TIPS

There is an old wives' tale to the effect that whenever parsley grows freely in a household, it signifies the wife wears the trousers! The plant is a biennial, or a short-lived perennial. Outdoors, seed is best sown in progression in late spring, summer, and early autumn in warm soil where it is to grow. Soaking the seed in lukewarm water speeds germination, while pouring boiling water along the seed drill both warms the soil and provides the necessary moisture. In winter, the plants should be protected by cloches or dug up and potted for overwintering indoors. If grown in pots and planters indoors – and it is an ideal candidate for this – the plants need a good potting soil, plenty of plant food and moisture, and eventually at least a 6-in/15-cm pot to allow for root development.

HOW TO USE

Parsley has its culinary uses in nearly every savory category of food, not only in garnishing but in preparing soups, sauces, and casseroles, in marinades, and with meat, poultry, fish, and vegetables. Often a sprig of parsley – surprisingly hard to come by unless you grow your own – is the only garnish needed to present a dish attractively.

The plant may be used for kidney complaints, as a tonic, and in the treatment of flatulence. An infusion splashed on the skin is said to lighten freckles and prevent thread veins, while the leaves provide a green or yellow dye.

SALSA VERDE

Ingredients
Serves 4
3 cloves of garlic, finely chopped
4 oz parsley, finely chopped
1 tbsp watercress leaves, finely chopped
(optional)
1 tbsp mixed fresh herbs, finely chopped
(basil, marjoram, and a little thyme, sage, chervil, and dill)
coarse salt
4 tbsp olive oil
juice of 1–2 lemons
1–2 tsp sugar
black pepper

Green and piquant, this sauce of fresh herbs is excellent with any fish and seafood, hot or cold, and also goes well with hard-cooked eggs.

Preparation
● Blend or pound in a mortar the garlic, parsley, watercress, fresh mixed herbs, and a little coarse salt until they form a smooth paste.
● Add the oil, a spoonful at a time, and mix well. Add the lemon juice and season with sugar, salt and pepper to taste.

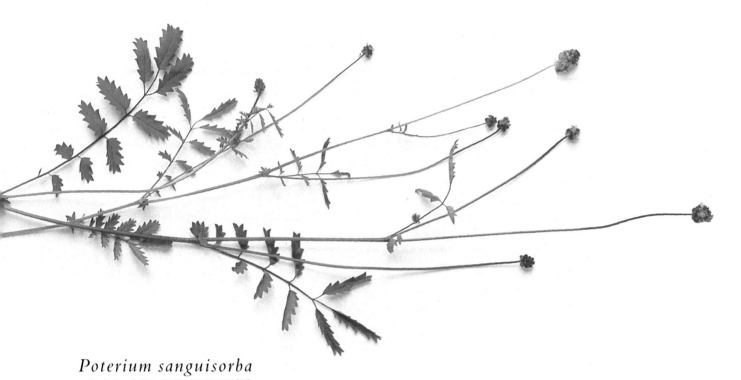

Poterium sanguisorba
SALAD BURNET

Burnet vinegar, a piquant addition to the range of salad dressing ingredients; burnet butter to drizzle over broiled fish or meats; and burnet leaves added sparingly, for their bitter-sweetness, to mixed green salads . . .

A popular herb in English cottage gardens, salad bur-net was taken to North America by the early colonists. It is native to Europe, where it grows on chalky soil, and particularly on the chalk downs of southern England. With their mild, cucumberlike flavor, the young leaves are useful in salads and, like borage, in ice-cold summer drinks. It is now mainly used in France and Italy, where it is frequently included in bunches of mixed salad leaves and herbs sold in markets.

HISTORY

Salad burnet, or lesser burnet (previously *Sanguisorba minor*), was a favorite salad herb in Elizabethan times, when the soft, blue-green leaves were prized for their "cool," mild flavor.

CHARACTERISTICS

The plant grows to a height of about 16 in/40 cm, with a spread of 9 in/23 cm. The small, heavily toothed, blue-green leaves are carried in pairs, widely spaced along the slender, curving stems. The red flowers, which appear in early summer, form small, spherical heads about ½ in/12 mm across.

GROWING TIPS

The plant, a herbaceous perennial, likes a chalky, well-drained soil and a sunny, sheltered position. It can be grown from seed planted in spring, or by root division in autumn. The leaves last well into winter and appear again in early spring, so it is virtually evergreen.

HOW TO USE

Fresh leaves may be used in salads, sauces, soups, and pâtés; in softened butter known as *ravigote*; steeped in vinegar for salad dressing; as a garnish; and in fruit salads and drinks. Medicinally, the fresh leaves act as a digestive. In self-help medicine, a decoction of the roots was used to stop bleeding, and an infusion of the leaves to cool sunburn.

ABOVE: Salad burnet plants are thick and bushy and tightly compact, their tiny red flowers towering above the leaves on long, slender stalks.

BELOW LEFT: A sprig of rosemary is the perfect addition to roast or broiled lamb. The herb dries well and retains its aroma over a long period.

BELOW: Rosemary, which grows into a thick, dense bush, likes a light, well-drained soil and a sheltered position.

Rosmarinus officinalis
ROSEMARY

Roast lamb with a generous sprig of rosemary pressed close against the sizzling skin; chopped rosemary in country-style sausages, giving them the flavor of Italy; soothing rosemary tea, taken ice-cold with lemon and honey . . .

An evergreen shrub, rosemary is available fresh year-round. This is just as well because, once dried, it loses much of its flavor, and its pine-needlelike leaves become unpalatably spiky. It is a pretty herb, with trusses of pale or bright blue flowers lasting, in the right climate, right through spring and summer. It is

native to the countries bordering the Mediterranean, where it grows in profusion, its slightly camphoric scent far more pronounced than it can ever be in cooler climatic conditions.

HISTORY

The name means dew (*ros*) of the sea (*marinus*) – the sea being the Mediterranean. In the Middle Ages in Britain, sprigs of rosemary were dipped in gold and tied with ribbon as a keepsake for wedding guests, and the herb was a traditional gift on New Year's day. Shakespeare immortalized its significance in the age-old language of flowers when Hamlet tells Ophelia, "There's rosemary, that's for remembrance."

CHARACTERISTICS

In the proper conditions, the bush can grow to a height of 6½ ft/2 m and spread 5 ft/1.5 m across. The leaves are dark green on top and silver-gray on the underside about 1 in/2.5 cm long and ⅛ in/3 mm wide. The two-lipped tubular flowers are small, about ½ in/ 12 mm long, and carried on long thick spikes. The stems become tough and woody.

GROWING TIPS

The plant is grown from tip cuttings taken in summer and set in sandy soil to take root. It prefers a light, well-drained soil and a sunny, sheltered position, and can be fan-trained against a wall, where it makes a most decorative spreading shrub. Pinch out the tip of the main shoot to encourage bushy side growth, and protect from frost and snow in winter.

HOW TO USE

Rosemary and lamb go together in many ways. Make slits in lamb for roasting and tuck in sprigs of the herb, place larger sprigs over chops for broiling, and include them in casseroles and stews. Use rosemary in bouquets garnis, sparingly with fish, and in rice dishes.

Medicinally, a tisane of the leaves is taken as a tonic for calming nerves, and is also used as an antiseptic. Use an infusion, too, as a rinse to lighten blond hair. The dried leaves are used in pot pourri and, in sachets, to scent clothes and linen.

CHICKPEA SOUP

Ingredients
Serves 4–6
4 cloves of garlic
½ tsp dried or 1 tsp fresh rosemary
4 tbsp olive oil
5 oz can plum tomatoes
1 lb can chickpeas, drained and rinsed
1 chicken stock cube
1¼ cups water
salt and pepper to taste

Preparation
• Peel and crush the garlic. If using fresh rosemary, chop it very finely.
• Heat the oil and sauté the garlic until it begins to brown. Add the rosemary and the tomatoes, roughly chopped, and lower the heat to a simmer when the ingredients come to a boil. Cook for 25 minutes or so.
• When the tomatoes are cooked, add the chickpeas and cook another 5 minutes.
• Stir in the stock cube and no more than 1¼ cups water. Season with salt and pepper to taste and serve.

Rumex scutatus
SORREL

Sorrel leaves gently torn and served as a piquant green salad with a built-in flavor; the leaves cooked as spinach, drained thoroughly and sprinkled with lemon juice; or lightly cooked to float in a clear broth in the Spanish style . . .

French sorrel, as it is known, is similar to spinach with lemony overtones, and so makes a distinctive and useful herb and vegetable. An herbaceous perennial, it is easy to grow, is always on hand, and has a variety of uses. And with its green-tipped-with-red flower spikes, it is decorative, too. In short, it earns its keep in any decorative or kitchen border.

HISTORY

Sorrel was used as a herb and vegetable in ancient Egypt, while the Greeks and Romans knew it, too, as an antidote to rich foods and fatty meats. It was popular in Britain during the Middle Ages, where it had both culinary and medicinal uses. A native of Europe and Asia, it was brought to England by the Romans and to America by the pilgrims.

CHARACTERISTICS

Sorrel can reach a height of 24 in/60 cm and a spread of 9 in/23 cm, though it is best used young, before it is fully matured and the long flower spikes form. The spinachlike leaves are deep dark green and shield shaped; they may be up to 6 in/15 cm long and 3 in/8 cm across. The flowers, which appear in late spring, are small, greenish red, and are borne on tall, loosely formed spikes.

GROWING TIPS

Seed is sown outdoors in midspring in a moist but well-drained soil, and should be thinned to 12 in/30 cm apart. A sunny or slightly shaded position is favored. The flowering stems should be removed to encourage leaf growth and prevent the plant running to seed, when the leaves become bitter.

HOW TO USE

The leaves may be cooked as a vegetable, drained well and dressed with oil and vinegar, cream, yogurt, or a dash of lemon juice. They are very good as salad, and make an unusual and delicious soup garnished with swirls of cream and garlic croutons. They are also used in lamb and beef casseroles, and to curdle milk and make junket.

OPPOSITE : For a
more abundant crop of
sorrel leaves, cut off the
decorative flower heads.

ABOVE : Sorrel leaves,
which are used in a
similar way to spinach,
have a pronounced
lemony flavor. They are
good with a vinaigrette
dressing.

POACHED SALMON WITH SORREL SAUCE

Ingredients
Serves 4
4 cutlets of salmon
¼ lb unsalted butter
1 large bunch of sorrel, washed and chopped
1¼ cups heavy cream or crème fraîche
salt and pepper

Preparation
• Poach the salmon in boiling salted water for about 8 minutes. Remove and set aside on a warm plate.
• Melt the butter in a saucepan. Add the chopped sorrel – it melts into the butter very quickly. When it has bubbled for a few minutes, add the cream and seasoning, bring to a boil and simmer for 10 minutes. If you are using crème fraîche, boil very rapidly for a few minutes.
• Pour the sauce over the salmon and serve immediately.

Ruta graveolens
RUE

The compact, tightly growing plants clipped to make an
attractive edging in a herb garden; the dried seedheads sprayed
gold for a sparkling Christmas decoration; or used in their
natural state, chestnut brown and shiny, in dried flower
arrangements . . .

Most herbs have retained their popularity over the
centuries not only because of their culinary and medicinal properties, but also their pleasant scent. That
cannot be said of rue, an herb whose aroma has been
likened, not unfairly, to the smell of tomcats. Accordingly, its culinary applications have not been enthusi-
astically handed down from one generation to the
next, while even its medicinal applications need
approaching with care.

Rue, a sub-shrub known as the herb of grace, is a
native of southern Europe, where it will flourish in the
poorest of soils. It will easily take to poor garden soil,
as well, where it makes a compact and decorative bush.

HISTORY

The ancient Greeks credited rue with the ability to
improve eyesight, and, in his herbal, Gerard took up
this theme, recommending it to be boiled, pickled,
and eaten "to quicken the sight."

CHARACTERISTICS

The bush can grow to 30 in/75 cm tall, with a width of
18 in/45 cm. The stems are tough and woody, while
the bluish green leaves are pointed oval, and deeply
divided. The flowers are bright yellow with four
petals, about ½ in/12 mm across, borne in loose clusters. The seedheads are chestnut brown, and look
rather like miniature wood carvings.

GROWING TIPS

The plant is grown from seed planted in spring or
from semi-hardwood cuttings taken under cover in
summer. It prefers poor, dry soil and plenty of sun.
The bush is a perfect candidate for clipping into decorative shapes. The variety 'Jackman's Blue' is possibly
the best known, and certainly the most attractive, with
its almost blue lacelike leaves.

HOW TO USE

The plant is not now used in the kitchen, and should
be approached with extreme care for medicinal purposes. The tisane – which was once taken for rheumatism, and used, much diluted, as an eye bath – is not
now recommended. Sprays of the leaves may be hung
indoors to repel insects.

The seedheads are particularly attractive, and can be
used in dried flower arrangements.

LEFT: With its thick clusters of gray-green downy leaves and its bright mauve or blue flowers, sage is an attractive border plant which is popular with bees.

BELOW: Sage leaves are strongly aromatic and are used sparingly in meat dishes of all kinds, particularly in stuffings and sausages.

Salvia officinalis
SAGE

Fresh sage leaves lightly fried in oil or butter to serve with veal escalope; sage and onion stuffing for the Christmas goose or roast of pork; dried purple sage leaves, an evergreen addition to a dried flower collection . . .

Sage is a decorative evergreen sub-shrub, though its leaves are not necessarily green. Some varieties have gray or gray-green downy leaves, and one has deep purple leaves and exceptionally pretty mauvy-blue flowers. The flavor, which has faint overtones of camphor, is very strong in some types, so making sage a herb to use little and often. The plant is a native of the Mediterranean region, where it thrives on poor, dry soil, and is especially important in Yugoslavia.

HISTORY

Sage, which takes its name from the Latin *salvere*, "to save," has a long history as a medicinal plant and was listed as such in Theophratus' works. It was much in

evidence in Roman times, again for medicinal purposes, but was well established mainly as a culinary herb in medieval England.

CHARACTERISTICS

The plant can reach a height of 2 ft/60 cm, with a spread of 18 in/45 cm. The stems are tough and woody, and the leaves, elongated ovals, can be 2½ in/6 cm long and ¾ in/2 cm across. The flowers, which appear in midsummer, are about 1 in/2.5 cm long, borne on long, curving clusters.

GROWING TIPS

Sage likes a well-drained soil and a sunny position. It can be grown from seed planted in spring, or from tip cuttings taken under cover in summer. Cuttings can also be rooted by layering. The plant tends to become woody and straggly, so should be renewed (by taking cuttings) every few years. Cutting off the stems before flowers form encourages leaf growth.

HOW TO USE

Sage is traditionally used in sauces and stuffings for fatty meats such as goose, duck, and pork, in bouquets garnis, and in sausages. In Italy the fresh leaves are lightly fried with liver, and rolled up with ham and veal in *saltimbocca*. In Germany and Belgium, sage leaves are added to eel and other oily fish dishes, while in some Middle Eastern countries they are liberally used in salads.

Medicinally, the leaves are used as an antiseptic and an astringent, while the tea is taken for sore throats and to calm the nerves. Sage leaves are strewn in bath water, and in the rinsing water when washing hair to strengthen dark coloring. Dried sage leaves are a frequent pot pourri ingredient.

ROAST STUFFED PORK STEAK

Ingredients
Serves 6
4 tbsp butter
1 onion, finely chopped
2 large cooking apples
1 handful of fresh sage and thyme, chopped
salt and pepper
2 lb cooked mashed potato
2 lb pork steak or fillet
2 tbsp butter
2 tbsp water or cider

Oven temperature: 350°F.

The classic marriage of pork and sage, cooked in a traditional Irish recipe.

Preparation
● Make the stuffing first. Add the butter, chopped onion, chopped apple, herbs, salt and pepper to the mashed potato. Mix well and check the seasoning.
● Place the meat in a ring shape in a casserole or roasting pan. Put the stuffing in the middle. Rub the meat with salt and butter and put a little water or cider in the pan, cover loosely with foil and cook in the oven for about 1 hour.
● Serve hot with the reduced pan juices, or cold, with roasted apples.

Salvia sclarea
CLARY

Used with elderflowers in winemaking to give it the flavor of muscatel; the fresh leaves used sparingly in robust soups and, in the medieval way, in light fritters to serve with just a sprinkling of sugar . . .

A native of southern Europe, clary was introduced into Britain in the sixteenth century, when it was used in brewing and combined with elderflowers to give wine the desired flavor of muscatel. It is a close relation of sage and a decorative biennial that is usually treated as an annual.

HISTORY

A sixteenth-century botanist said of clary that "it re-stores the natural heat, and comforts the vital spirits, and helps the memory." At the same time, the leaves were used in omelets, boiled with cream, and made into fritters to serve with orange or lemon juice.

CHARACTERISTICS

Clary grows to a height of 3 ft/90 cm, with a spread of about 12 in/30 cm. It has oval, downy, dark green leaves, which can be up to 8 in/20 cm long. The flower bracts, about 2 in/5 cm long, may be mauve, pink, or white, and are carried on straight, branching spikes at the top of the plant; the bracts are purple or pink. The fragrance is somewhat balsamic, the taste bitter.

GROWING TIPS

The plant is grown from seed planted in spring, and will flower the following year. It requires a light soil and a warm, sheltered position if it is to survive the rigors of winter.

HOW TO USE

The strongly aromatic leaves can be added sparingly in the preparation of soups, casseroles, homemade wines and beer, or made into fritters. Medicinally, they may be used to make a gargle or mouthwash, as an anti-septic, and a skin cleanser. Clary's derived name, clear eye, suggests it was also used to concoct an eye bath.

A B O V E : Clary, with its thick, rounded leaves and papery bracts, is a close relation of sage. Its name is derived from the folkloric term, clear eye.

A B O V E   L E F T : With its stout, sturdy stems and reaching a height of 3 ft/90 cm, clary is a vigorous plant which looks well in an herbaceous border.

Sambucus nigra
ELDER

Trusses of fluffy cream flowers used to make a country-style non-alcoholic "champagne," or a sparkling wine, or strewn with gooseberries to enhance the flavor of pies, custards and compotes; the succulent berries used for wine or, with apples, a homemade jam . . .

In springtime, the aroma of the umbrella-like trusses of creamy-white elderflowers scents the hedgerows and country lanes with a sweet aroma one longs to capture. The plant is common throughout Europe, western Asia, and North America, where a related species, *S. canadensis*, American elder, was used as a folk medicine by the American Indians.

HISTORY

Elder has attracted a strong folk history. It was thought that a tree planted outside a house kept witches at bay and protected the house from lightning. Cutting it back was said to bring bad luck.

CHARACTERISTICS

The tree can grow to a height of about 30 ft/10 m or more, with a spread of 9 ft/2.5 m, but many trees are much smaller. The leaves are dull dark green, about 4 in/10 cm long and finely toothed. The flowers are minute, highly fragrant, and carried in umbel-like clusters. The purplish black berries are small and round, and hang in heavy trusses.

GROWING TIPS

The trees like a moist soil and plenty of sun if the flowers are to develop their maximum fragrance. Elders are grown from hardwood cuttings taken outdoors in the autumn.

HOW TO USE

Elder flowers are traditionally used to flavor fruit compotes, salads, and gelatin desserts, and have an affinity with gooseberries. The berries – usually blended with apples – can be made into jam, jelly, and other preserves, while both flowers and berries create excellent wines. The flowers, blended with lemon and sugar, are used to flavor summer drinks and cordials. Elderberry soup (again, mixed with apples) is a popular Scandinavian dish.

Elderflower water is widely used, and sold commercially, as a skin toner and lightener.

ELDERFLOWER "CHAMPAGNE"

Ingredients
Yields 1 gal
1 gal water
3½ cups sugar
1 juicy lemon
4 large elderflower heads
2 tbsp white wine vinegar

Serve the champagne chilled as a fragrant, refreshing summer drink.

Preparation
● Warm a little of the water, then stir in the sugar until it has dissolved. Leave to cool. Squeeze the juice from the lemon, then cut the rind into 4 pieces, discarding the pith.
● Put the flowers into a large, non-metallic container, add the pieces of lemon rind, the sweetened water, remaining water and the vinegar. Stir, then cover and leave for 4–5 days.
● Strain off the liquid and pour into clean screw-top bottles. Leave for 6 days, by which time it should be effervescent. If it is not, leave for up to another 4 days.

ABOVE: Elderflowers are used to make wine and non-alcoholic summer drinks, and to flavor syrups, sweet sauces and creams. They have a special affinity with gooseberries.

OPPOSITE: Elderflower's umbrella-like trusses of minute cream flowers are pleasantly aromatic, and scent the hedgerows in late spring.

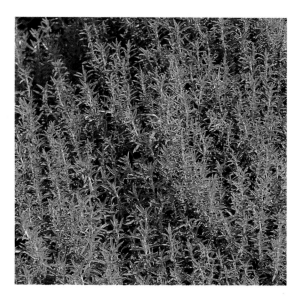

Satureja hortensis
SUMMER SAVORY
S. montana
WINTER SAVORY

The first of the young and tender lima beans sprinkled with the first of the young and tender summer savory leaves; the leaves of winter savory added to a bouquet garni to use in meat or vegetable casseroles . . .

Summer savory, a half-hardy annual that self-sows freely, has a strong, hot and slightly bitter flavor reminiscent of thyme, and retains a particular affinity with peas and beans, lima beans especially.

Winter savory is a shrubby perennial with a similar, though somewhat stronger, flavor that was at one time frequently used with trout and other oily fish.

HISTORY

Both types of herb originate from the Mediterranean region, and were much in demand by the Romans, who introduced them to Britain. Savory was said to be a stimulant and, as such, was thought to be an effective aphrodisiac.

CHARACTERISTICS

Summer savory grows to a height of 18 in/45 cm and 6 in/15 cm across. It has an untidy, straggling habit. The leaves are long, narrow, and dark green, rather like soft pine needles. Its flowers are small, pale mauve, and insignificant, and bloom well into the autumn. Winter savory grows to a height of some 12 in/30 cm, and has a spread of around 8 in/20 cm. The leaves are grayish green and similar to those of summer savory, while the flowers, borne in spiky clusters, are pinky white or pink.

GROWING TIPS

Summer savory is grown from seed planted in late spring; it likes a light soil and a sunny, sheltered position. The seed of winter savory is planted in late summer, in warm soil outdoors when it will quickly germinate. It enjoys poor soil and plenty of sun.

HOW TO USE

Summer savory is used with pork and game, in soups, sausages, pâtés, and stuffings, in bouquets garnis, and with vegetables, particularly fresh and dried peas and beans. Winter savory has similar uses, but its stronger flavor is considered inferior. Both herbs may be used as a tonic and a digestive, and are said to ease insect bites and stings.

Symphytum officinale COMFREY

The very young leaves chopped and stirred into cream cheese for spreads or lightly cooked, tossed in melted butter and eaten as a vegetable; the roots used as a flavoring for a range of country wines . . .

Its somewhat comforting name points to the fact that, in medieval times, comfrey had so many self-help medicinal applications it was looked upon almost as a cure-all. Its popular country name, knit-bone, describes one of them: when the ground root was moistened and applied to a broken joint, the resulting composition set like plaster.

Comfrey is a native of Asia and Europe and it grows freely in temperate regions of North America. Indeed, it grows freely wherever it grows at all, attaining rampant weed proportions if not contained.

HISTORY

The roots and leaves were applied to swellings, sprains, bruises, and cuts, and as a poultice to abscesses, boils, and stings.

CHARACTERISTICS

The plant, a perennial, has dull, dark green, hairy leaves, which may be up to 8 in/20 cm long; they have no aroma, and are not in the least attractive. The bell-shaped flowers are cream flashed with red, and hang in clusters. The roots are thick, tapering, and persistently multiply. The plant grows to 3 ft/90 cm tall, with a spread of 18 in/45 cm.

GROWING TIPS

One plant, or even a piece of root with or without a shoot, is all that is needed to establish a patch of comfrey. Root divisions may be made at any time except during January and February. Plant the piece of root in deep, moist soil; the roots can penetrate to at least 3 ft/90 cm. With a high concentration of potash, the plants provide a natural source of nutrition for the soil.

HOW TO USE

Comfrey is related to borage, and can be used in similar ways. The young leaves can be cooked and eaten as spinach. A cleansing skin oil may be made by steeping young leaves in good-quality oil, such as almond oil, while the leaves and stalks produce a pale yellow dye.

LEFT: Comfrey plants are energetic colonizers, and one piece of root will soon develop into a large patch.

BELOW: The trusses of mauvey-pink flowers which last throughout the summer compensate for the dense green lack-lustre leaves of the comfrey plant.

Tanacetum vulgare
TANSY

Bunches of the small golden-ball flowers hanging decoratively in room corners to dry or providing the colorful focal point in dried flower arrangements; and the flower name given to the medieval dishes of creams, custards and possets . . .

Tansy is a native of Europe and also grows wild in the eastern United States, where it is cultivated commercially. It was a common cottage-garden herb in medieval times, when it was used as an insect repellent, a strewing herb, and as a source of orange dye.

HISTORY

During the Middle Ages, the strong, bitter, and some say unpleasant, flavor of the leaves was no barrier to the herb's use in salads, desserts, and cakes, while tansy pancakes, which included thyme, marjoram, and parsley, were a traditional feasting dish at Eastertime.

CHARACTERISTICS

A large but graceful plant, tansy can grow to 3 ft/ 90 cm tall, with a spread of some 2 ft/60 cm. It has dark green pinnate leaves about 6 in/15 cm long, and umbel-like clusters of small, dome-shaped flowers, bright, deep yellow and very attractive.

GROWING TIPS

The plant is a herbaceous perennial, grown by root division in spring or autumn, or from seed sown in spring. It likes a dry, well-drained soil and a sunny outdoor position.

HOW TO USE

The use of tansy leaves in desserts was once so widespread that "tansy" became the generic name for baked or boiled egg custard flavored by infusing the leaves. It may be used in salads, egg dishes, and casseroles, but only in small quantities. In self-help medicine, the leaves were used as a digestive. Note, the herb should not be taken during pregnancy.

The flowers may be hung in a dry, airy place and used in dried flower arrangements. The dried leaves act as a powerful insect repellent, and were "put up in bags" for this purpose.

TANSY & BEEF CASSEROLE

Ingredients
Serves 6
3 tbsp oil
2 lb braising steak, cut into 1½ in cubes
6 oz bacon, diced
2 large onions, finely chopped
1 clove of garlic, crushed
3 large tomatoes, peeled, seeds removed and chopped
2 cups beef stock
2 cups red wine
3–4 tbsp finely chopped tansy (use
Tanacetum vulgare only – not to be taken during pregnancy)
salt and freshly ground black pepper
Oven temperature: 300°F.

Preparation
● Heat 2 tbsp oil in a heavy ovenproof casserole, add the beef and bacon in batches, and cook over a moderately high heat, stirring occasionally, until evenly browned. Remove each batch using a slotted spoon and drain on paper towels.
● When all the meat has cooked, add the remaining oil to the pan, then stir in the onions, garlic, and tomatoes, and cook over a low heat, stirring occasionally, until the onion is soft.
● Return the meat to the pan, stir in the stock and wine and bring to simmering point. Add the tansy, salt, and plenty of black pepper. Cover the casserole tightly (use foil if the lid is not a close fit), and place in the oven for about 2 hours, stirring occasionally, until the meat is very tender.
● Strain off the liquid and boil until reduced to about 1¼ – 1½ cups. Keep the meat warm while the liquid is being boiled. Check the seasoning, then return the meat for a minute or two. Serve with some tansy sprinkled over the top.

NB: Use *Tanacetum vulgare* only – not to be taken in pregnancy.

ABOVE: Tansy leaves have a strong, pungent aroma. Use *Tanacetum vulgare* only – and sparingly – in cooking; it should not be taken at all during pregnancy. The flowers dry well and are attractive in long-lasting arrangements.

OPPOSITE: With its bright green leaves and large clusters of golden-yellow flowers, tansy makes a colorful impact in an herbaceous border.

Taraxacum officinale
DANDELION

The bright green young leaves as tender as can be for a salad or, lightly cooked, as a vegetable; the flowers used to make a dry light wine, to a generations-old country recipe . . .

Dandelion, native to Europe and Asia, is a herbaceous perennial that has become a rampant weed, its bright yellow flowers intruding on many a lawn and well-tended flower border. Its common name comes from the French *dent de lion,* "lion's tooth," signifying the toothed appearance of the leaves. Its more colloquial names – piss-a-beds in English, *pis-en-lit* in French – bear witness to its strong diuretic properties.

HISTORY

In medieval times dandelion was used as a mild laxative, a diuretic, a tonic, and in the treatment of liver complaints. The juice of the plant was used in a folkloric treatment of warts.

CHARACTERISTICS

The plant has a persistent root system that, for those who do not appreciate the plant's qualities, is difficult to eradicate. The plant reaches a height of 12 in/30 cm. The leaves, which may be up to 8 in/20 cm long and 2 in/5 cm across, are bright, sharp lettuce green,

attractive, and appetizing in appearance. The flowers bloom eight or nine months of the year, are made up of a mass of florets, and measure about 1½ in/3.5 cm across. The seeds form a fluffy ball, known as a clock, which in days past used to be the subject of a children's chanting game.

GROWING TIPS

More people are interested in how to eliminate dandelions than to grow them. All you need is the smallest piece of root generously donated by a neighbor, and you will have dandelions forever.

HOW TO USE

The young leaves, high in vitamins and minerals, make an excellent salad, delicious with a slightly lemony dressing. They may also be lightly cooked like spinach, when they are good served with vinaigrette. The ground and roasted root is dried and used as a caffeine-free coffee substitute. The leaves and root are used to give a bitter flavor to country beers such as nettle and burdock, and a stout is made from the roots. Both the flowers and leaves are used, separately, to make wines.

Dandelion is valued as a medicinal herb for all urinary troubles. The roots produce a yellow or crimson dye, according to the mordant used.

LEFT: A patch of several varieties of thyme shows how varied and attractive this versatile herb can be.

BELOW: The tiny mauve thyme flowers have a stronger, sweeter aroma than the leaves and can be widely used in cooking.

Thymus vulgaris
GARDEN THYME

Creamy golden thyme sauce with fish; garden thyme oil for salad dressings; fragrant lemon thyme leaves strewn in custards and creams . . .

Thyme is a sun-loving herb, at its aromatic best when growing wild on the sun-baked hills around the Mediterranean. Grown in the garden in less favorable climates, it will be aromatic, but less powerfully so. It is a decorative herb, covered for two or three of the summer months with delicate pale mauve flowers, themselves highly fragrant, attractive to bees, and with many culinary uses. Different species offer a range of flavors: try *T. citriodorus,* lemon thyme, for a distinctly citrus aroma, and *T. herba-barona,* caraway thyme, for a spicy flavor. The English wild thyme referred to by Shakespeare is *T. drucei.*

HISTORY

Thyme is one of the oldest recorded culinary herbs, probably in use well before the time of the ancient

Greeks. The Romans took it to Britain as part of their culinary armory. In his herbal, Nicholas Culpeper credits it with a singular usefulness: "An infusion of the leaves," he has written, "removes the headache occasioned by inebriation."

CHARACTERISTICS

Thyme is a low-growing sub-shrub that can become untidily woody and straggly. It can reach a height and spread of about 8 in/20 cm. The leaves are very small, only about ¼ in/6 mm long; according to type, they may be green, gray-green, yellow, or variegated. The flowers, which cover the plant from early summer, are borne in clusters at the tips of the shoots.

GROWING TIPS

Thyme thrives on poor, stony soil as long as it is planted in full sun; in an indoor situation, this means a south-facing windowsill. It is grown from tip cuttings taken in summer, or by layering stems. It will need

protection in a harsh winter. Wild creeping thyme, *T. pulegioides,* is planted as a flowering lawn.

HOW TO USE

Thyme is traditionally used with parsley in stuffings for chicken and pork, and, with the addition of a bay leaf, in bouquets garnis for use in soups and casseroles. It is especially good with oil and wine or vinegar in marinades for meat and fish, and with vegetables such as zucchini, eggplant, sweet peppers, and tomatoes. It both dries and freezes well, so no kitchen need ever be without it. Lemon thyme may be used in custards, fruit salads, and syrups.

The essential oil – thymol – is a strong antiseptic. Thus an infusion may be used as a mouthwash, a gargle, and a wash for cuts and abrasions. The dried leaves, especially those of lemon thyme, are used to scent linen, and are an important ingredient in pot pourri, herb, and sleep pillows.

BEEF BRAISED IN BAROLO

Ingredients
Serves 6
2 tbsp olive oil
1 beef roast of about 2 lb
1 cup *tritto* (finely diced vegetables – onions, carrots, celery – mixed with herbs and steeped in olive oil for at least 12 hours)
1¼ cups Barolo or other dry red wine
1¼ cups beef stock
1¼ cups fresh or canned plum tomatoes
1 tsp each of thyme and marjoram
salt to taste
Oven temperature: 350°F.

Preparation
● Preheat the oven. Heat the oil over a medium flame and brown the beef roast. Seal it on all sides, then set aside.
● Now add the *tritto* to the beef pan and cook it until soft, 3–4 minutes.
● Transfer the beef to a casserole a little larger than the beef itself. Retrieve the *tritto* with a slotted spoon – without the oil. Spread it over and around the beef. Pour in the wine, the stock, and the tomatoes; add the herbs.
● Put the beef in the oven, covered with a well-fitting lid. Turn the roast completely over at half time. Check the liquid content from time to time; add more water if necessary. If by the end of the cooking time the sauce is too thin, thicken it by means of reducing.
● To serve, carve the beef and spoon the sauce over, checking for salt before you do.

Trigonella foenum-graecum
FENUGREEK

The green leaves curried as a spicy and piquant vegetable; the seeds roasted and pounded as a curry spice or, straight from the plant, sprouted and eaten at the two-leaf stage as a hot and tasty salad . . .

Fenugreek, which takes its name from the Latin for Greek hay, has been grown as an animal fodder crop around the Mediterranean region since ancient times. But it is much more valuable and versatile than that. The sprouting seeds may be eaten at the cotyledon stage as a spicy salad; the fully developed leaves, too bitter to cook as spinach, are served in the Indian way, as a curry; and the lightly roasted seeds are used as a spice, also principally in curries. The ground seeds, containing coumarin, are a major ingredient in commercially prepared curry powders.

HISTORY

The plant is a native of western Asia and has been widely grown in countries bordering the Mediterranean, particularly in Egypt. Its cultivation in northern Europe was principally intended for forage, to mix with hay crops.

CHARACTERISTICS

The plant, a half-hardy annual, bears some resemblance to lucerne. It grows to a height of 2 ft/60 cm, with a spread of 8 in/20 cm. The leaves are trefoil, rather like clover, and the flowers, which appear in late spring, are cream or pale yellow and vetchlike. The seed is compact and pale brown. Light roasting brings out the full flavor.

GROWING TIPS

The seed may be sown indoors in midspring or outdoors in warm soil in late spring. Fenugreek likes a good, well-drained soil and a position in full sun, which is essential if the seed is to set.

HOW TO USE

The sprouted seeds are good as a salad, tossed in a vinaigrette dressing. The roasted seeds are used in Middle Eastern variations of *halva*, a rich sweetmeat, as well as in curries. Medicinally, an infusion of the seeds may be taken for flatulence. The seed produces a yellow dye.

BELOW: The fenugreek plant grows to a height of 2 ft/60 cm. The spicy and pungent seeds are used in curries and may be sprouted, when the leaves are eaten as a salad.

ABOVE: Nettles, which grow as a vigorous and rampant weed, are attractive to bees and butterflies and are frequently grown for this reason.

Urtica dioica
NETTLE

Tall, ungainly nettle plants a haven for butterflies and moths; the young, tender leaves made into a nutritious and tasty soup to swirl with cream or cooked, as spinach, to serve with a twist of lemon . . .

The main excuse of many a gardener who has not cleared a patch of stinging nettles is that he has left them for the butterflies and moths, who feed on them voraciously. And the main excuse of many a cook who leaves an unsightly cluster of nettles is that he likes them in soup.

HISTORY

It is said that the Roman soldiers tolerated stinging nettles to keep them warm during long marches in their northern territories.

CHARACTERISTICS

The plants, herbaceous perennials, can grow to a dreary-looking 6 ft/1.8 cm tall, with a spread of 12 in/30 cm. The roots are tough and persistent, and extremely hard to eradicate. The leaves are dull green, matte, sharply toothed, and covered in hairs, which break off when touched, leaving formic acid and a burning sensation on the skin. The greenish yellow flowers are minute and insignificant, and are carried in curving trusses like miniature catkins.

GROWING TIPS

No one ever plants nettles: they just arrive, and they come to stay. All you need to start a colony is a piece of root with an eye.

HOW TO USE

The young leaves are good lightly cooked like spinach, and in soup garnished with croutons and cream. They are also used to make beer. In self-help medicine the leaves were used to treat rheumatism, as a diuretic, and as a soothing aid to skin problems. The root fiber was at one time used to make twine, and bunches of fresh leaves were hung in the home to deter flies.

LEFT: Young stinging nettle leaves are used to make beer, and are lightly cooked as spinach. They are delicious both as a vegetable and in soup.

Verbascum thapsus
MULLEIN

The long, erect spires of yellow flowers, the tallest pride and joy of the herbaceous border; the woolly silver-gray leaves providing clusters of neutral color and, in days gone by, the wherewithal for a range of self-help medicines . . .

With its tall, stately spires of primrose-yellow flowers, mullein is likely to be one of the tallest and most attractive plants in the border. It is a native of Europe and Asia, and grows wild in Britain and North America. It was a familiar plant in cottage gardens, where it had a number of folk names, including torches, hag taper, Adam's flannel, and Aaron's rod.

HISTORY

The plant has a long association with witchcraft, and it is said that witches used the down on the leaves to make potions. One of the folkloric names refers to the fact that the stems were dipped in tallow after flowering and used as torches by the Greeks and Romans.

CHARACTERISTICS

The erect, central-flowering stems can reach a height of 6½ ft/2 m and more. The pale yellow flowers are tightly packed around the stem, covering it with color. The leaves are gray-green and woolly, and can be up to 12 in/30 cm long.

GROWING TIPS

Mullein is a biennial, grown from seed planted in warm soil in spring. It enjoys a light, well-drained soil and a sunny position.

HOW TO USE

The plant is not fragrant and has no culinary uses. In folk medicine the leaves were used to treat coughs, catarrh and asthma, and were a mild sedative. The dried flowers are infused in water to make a lightening hair rinse. If the leaves are used in an infusion, it must first be strained through a fine cloth to remove the minute hairs.

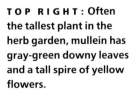

TOP RIGHT: Often the tallest plant in the herb garden, mullein has gray-green downy leaves and a tall spire of yellow flowers.

ABOVE: In folkloric medicine, mullein leaves were used in an infusion to relieve coughs, catarrh and asthma.

ABOVE RIGHT: Vervain leaves have no culinary uses but may be made into a tisane which is a soothing bedtime drink and may help to alleviate nervous conditions.

RIGHT: Vervain, which forms a dense, compact plant, likes a good, well-drained soil and plenty of sun.

Verbena officinalis
VERVAIN

The yellowish green leaves with a folkloric reputation as a love potion and, more recently, as an ingredient in liqueurs; an infusion of the leaves taken in self-help medicine to act as a mild sedative . . .

A native of the Mediterranean region, vervain now grows wild on waste ground and by the wayside in Europe and North America. Although it has no culinary uses, it has a long history of medicinal applications, particularly in the treatment of nervous disorders.

HISTORY

The plant was once considered virtually a cure-all, as well as a powerful aphrodisiac, and Culpeper listed many claimed remedies in his herbal. Vervain was also associated with witchcraft and believed to have magical powers.

CHARACTERISTICS

A herbaceous perennial, vervain grows to a height of 3 ft/90 cm and may be 18 in/45 cm across. It has fibrous, spreading roots and hairy, branching stems. The yellowish green, toothed leaves are up to about 2 in/5 cm long. The flowers, borne at the tips of the shoots, are small, mauve, and insignificant.

GROWING TIPS

Vervain is grown from seed planted in spring or from tip cuttings taken in summer. The roots can be divided in spring or autumn. It likes a good, well-drained soil and plenty of sun.

HOW TO USE

The tisane made from the fresh or dried leaves is a mild sedative, a soothing bedtime drink. The infusion may be taken to alleviate nervous conditions and depression, and to aid digestion. In self-help medicine, a diluted infusion was used as an eye bath to sooth inflamed and sore eyes.

Index

Page numbers in *italic* refer to picture captions